KNACK
MAKE IT EASY

MAGIC TRICKS

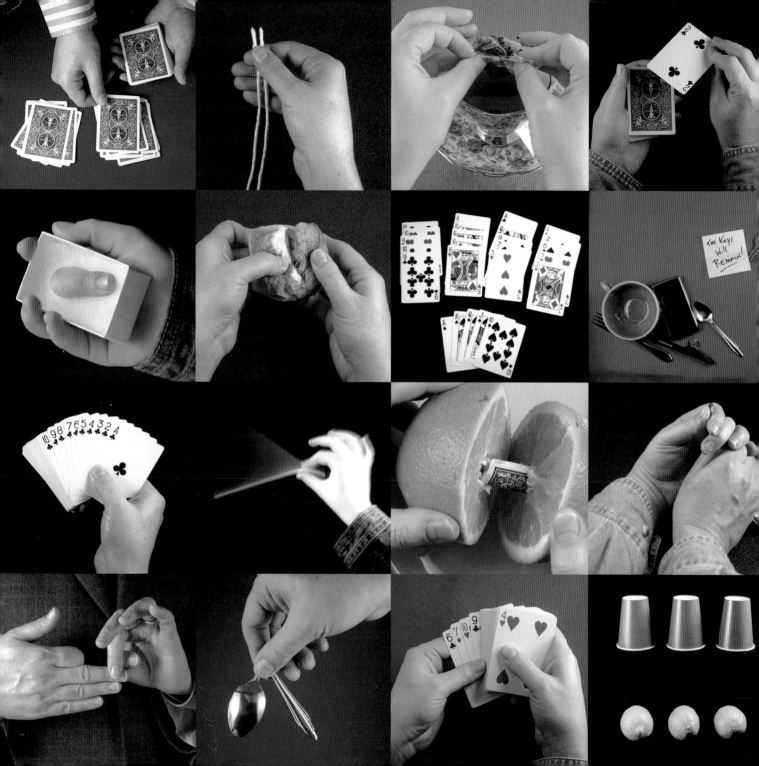

KNACK

MAGIC TRICKS

A Step-by-Step Guide to Illusions, Sleight of Hand, and Amazing Feats

RICHARD KAUFMAN

Photography by Elizabeth Kaufman

Foreword by David Copperfield

KNACK
MAKE IT EASY

Guilford, Connecticut
An imprint of Globe Pequot Press

KNACK®
MAKE IT EASY

Editor-in-Chief: Maureen Graney
Editors: Keith Wallman, Imee Curiel
Cover Design: Paul Beatrice, Bret Kerr
Text Design: Paul Beatrice
Layout: Melissa Evarts
Cover and interior photographs by Elizabeth Kaufman
Special photo treatments by Lori Enik
All posters courtesy The Nielsen Magic Poster Collection

Library of Congress Cataloging-in-Publication Data

Kaufman, Richard.
  Knack magic tricks : a step-by-step guide to illusions, sleights of hand, and amazing feats / Richard Kaufman ; photography by Elizabeth Kaufman ; foreword by David Copperfield.
      p. cm.
  Includes index.
  ISBN 978-1-59921-779-6
  1. Magic tricks—Juvenile literature. I. Title. II. Title: Magic tricks.
  GV1548.K38 2010
  793.8—dc22

                                    2009032236

Printed in China

10 9 8 7 6 5 4 3 2 1

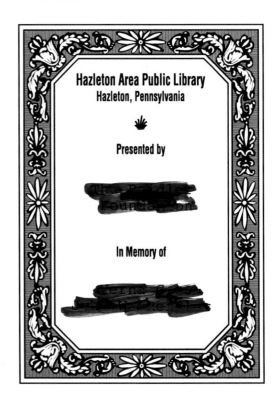

For my father, my wife, and my daughter: the past, the present, and the future. At this wonderful point in time we are all able to link hands and hearts to create real magic.

Acknowledgments

My interest in magic began at age five and was inspired by a gift of simple tricks from my aunt and uncle, Alan and Megan Soffin. This was followed several Christmases later by my uncle's subsequent gift of some magic books, which I own and treasure to this day. My parents, Lewis and Linda, encouraged my interest, with my father making a clandestine trip to a magic shop in Manhattan to buy and learn some simple tricks, which he then proceeded to teach me on a happily remembered Sunday morning at a Greek coffee shop in Queens, where we lived (in Queens, not in the coffee shop). Then there was the Great Maurice (from exotic Brooklyn!), wearing a red fez, teaching magic at Creative Day Camp in Valley Stream, Long Island. These were my first inspirations and mentors, and for many reasons the most important.

As I grew up in the world of magic many new friends encouraged me, including Señor Mardo, Gene Maze, Harry Lorayne, Bob Elliott, Sol Stone, Derek Dingle, Slydini, Alan Greenberg, and, later, Dai Vernon, Larry Jennings, and Brother John Hamman. I cannot imagine another area of the performing arts where a shy kid would be readily welcomed and encouraged by adults who were at the top of their field. Some of these friends are now long dead, but the simple act of writing a book such as *Knack Magic Tricks* allows me to continue their generosity and initiate you into the grand tradition of sharing our secrets with those who are genuinely interested. If you're even reading this part of the book, you've already passed the test.

I must thank those magicians who created the wonderful tricks that fill the pages of this book, those both anonymous—whose names have been lost to time—and those whom I'm happily able to credit for their ingenious ideas. I have adapted many of these tricks to make them simpler and fit the Knack format; however, my own tinkering in no way dilutes the value of their original inventors' ingenuity.

In particular I'm indebted to Jim Steinmeyer, without whom I would never have had the opportunity to write this book, and who, when I got stuck, always answered my not-so-smart questions with very smart answers. My friend Max Maven, whose encyclopedic mind proved to be of invaluable assistance on past projects, also helped by providing important information on several occasions. Gabe Fajuri and Bill Kalush also provided helpful historical information.

Finally, I must thank my lovely wife Liz, who took three thousand photos of a very grumpy subject, all the while doing a great job and maintaining good humor.

I've been aided greatly in all of this by the sage advice, patience, and support of my editors Keith Wallman, Imee Curiel, Katie Benoit, and Knack editor-in-chief Maureen Graney. I'm an old dog, and they've taught me a few new tricks. This is my attempt to teach some to you.

CONTENTS

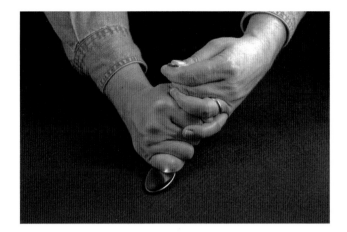

FOREWORD

Does the world really need another book about how to do magic? Perhaps. While there have been many, this one has been created and written by a real writer and teacher who knows magic inside out. I've known Richard Kaufman for over thirty years, during which he has written or published many of the most famous books in the world of magic. Some of the most prominent magicians in the world have chosen him to record their finest mysteries in print for future generations.

When the time came to pick someone to write the textbook for my organization, Project Magic, which teaches people in hospitals—both kids and adults—how to regain physical and mental abilities through the learning of magic, I chose Richard. His work is superb.

We first met at the opposite ends of a magic shop in New York City in our teens, but I was interested in theater and magic for the stage, and he was interested in close-up magic. Our paths have brought us together many times, sometimes in articles for his magazine, *Genii* (the oldest independent magazine in the world devoted to magic), and other times when he visits my museum in Nevada to do research for one of his many projects.

One thing that both Richard and I know well is that magic is about more than just doing a trick and fooling someone. It literally grants you a power that no one else in your social circle will have. It's an immediate introduction, an attention

getter, an ice breaker, a really quick way to immediately socialize a group of people into having a shared experience of amazement. As the person doing the "amazing," you'll find that your life will change and your friends will look at you with a bit more fascination and interest than ever before.

Enjoy.

David Copperfield

INTRODUCTION

What is "magic," and why have I written this book? It's an ancient performing art, presenting apparent impossibilities, that is at least as old as the Egyptians who built the pyramids. But "magic" is also, in its simplest form, a trick: something that involves a secret that is known to the performer but not to the audience. Some tricks work by themselves (even good ones, which may come as a surprise to you), whereas others require decades of practice and a lifetime of devotion to perform properly. But those are the extremes—there is an enormous amount of magic that falls into a middle area that requires a little bit of work on your part. After years of involvement with professional magicians, sharing their secrets, I've always wanted to write a book on magic for non-magicians. Here's where we make it all easy for you with the wonderful format of the Knack series. Now, with the instructions broken down into only the most essential information, combined with large color photographs that lead you step by step through each action, you'll find that learning magic is easier than you thought possible.

I've been very fortunate, in the past thirty years of writing and publishing books about magic and editing *Genii, The Conjurors' Magazine,* to have befriended many of the most brilliant people in the field. I have asked them, and they have generously agreed, to allow some of their most wonderful magic to be described for you in these pages. In the past, these tricks have appeared in print exclusively for magicians, and this is the first time they are being taught outside of our field. When combined with lucid explanations of some classic effects to which I've added a few interesting touches, these tricks are guaranteed to have your friends thinking you've been practicing for years or secretly learning how to read minds and predict the future. This installment in the Knack series has provided me with a long-sought opportunity to make magic easy to learn.

The most significant thing anyone has ever told me about magic was a concise bit of advice from one of the best magicians in the world, David Berglas. The British magician, now in his eighties, states this very succinctly: "The most important things in the performance of magic are personality, presentation, effect, and method—in that order." So, what exactly does Berglas's professional advice mean in general, and what does it mean specifically for you, a budding magician? Let's look at these in backward order, from least important to most.

"Method" is exactly what it sounds like—the secret of the trick. It's the physical thing that must be done in order to make a magic trick function. Most beginners think that the secret is the most important part of a trick—it's the thing they want to know immediately when a trick fools them. The biggest secret of magic, the secret that people really don't want to tell you, is that the method is the **least** important component in the successful performance of magic.

"Effect" is a word you may have heard before, but in this case it's really magician's jargon for "what a trick looks like to the audience." In other words, if you make a handkerchief disappear, that's an "effect." "Trick" and "effect" are synonyms.

"Presentation" is what you, as a performer, do to make the effect interesting to the audience. Without "presentation," an effect is merely a puzzle. For example: A person who doesn't speak and has no expression on his face places a coin on his palm. He closes and then opens his fingers, and the coin is gone. That's a puzzle because there's nothing entertaining and magical about it—it's a demonstration of a method, which usually leads the person watching to interpret this as a challenge to figure it out. Puzzles are not magical. "Presentation" does not consist solely of the words you say when performing a trick but also of your manner, the expressions on your face, your body language and movements, and the following element . . .

"Personality" is something that you already know. It's you—the way your voice, mannerisms, body movements, and that special something that makes you interesting all come together to create your personality. What many magicians, even professionals, sometimes forget is that they are not in front of an audience to present a puzzle and that the trick itself is not the thing that will make the performance a memorable event. **Your personality is the most important part of the performance of magic.** The trick is merely a vehicle to display your personality. Although you don't find it difficult to let your personality show in everyday life, you will find that it wants to hide when you start to perform magic—the secret is to let it out.

Back to "what is magic?" in a more specific sense. There are really three types of presentations: "close-up," where the magician stands beside you and does tricks under your nose (and for a group of people of about half a dozen); "parlor" or "stand-up," where the magician is standing in front of a group of people in a room but not on a large stage; and "illusion," where the magician—someone like David Copperfield—is doing big tricks on a big stage. This book deals with "close-up" and "stand-up" magic, if for no other reason than the most practical: The illusions you see magicians perform on stage often cost tens of thousands of dollars. Close-up and stand-up magic, however, can be performed with items that are easily found around your house. Even if you had to purchase everything needed to perform all the tricks in this book, it would cost less than $100. And considering the number of shows you could perform with all these tricks, that's pretty remarkable! And that's one of the great things about magic as both a hobby and a profession—you don't have to spend a lot of money unless you want to.

You may be wondering, if you've been paying attention to magic on TV or the Internet for the past ten years, where the category of "street magic" is in the preceding paragraph. It's not there because there is no such thing—it's a marketing ploy. Street magic is simply close-up magic done while standing outside. If you want to do so-called street magic, there are dozens of tricks in this book that are perfectly suited to performance outside.

Finally, the only thing that stands between a magician's triumph and an amateur's embarrassment is often the secret of the trick. That's why you hear silly things about magicians having some sort of "secret code." This is nonsense. There's a practical reason not to tell anyone how you do a trick: The method is not impressive. The mechanics are simple. **The effect is only impressive if the method remains a secret:** People don't realize that magic is just a nuts-and-bolts sequence of events (like any other learned technique, such as fly fishing or cooking). When you perform a trick, do it well, and you'll be amazed at people's reactions—you will be elevated in their eyes. Tell them how it's done and they'll wonder why you're wasting your time with something so silly.

Magician's sleeves are always blue denim.

Spectator's sleeves are always striped.

So, don't tell anyone how you do a trick—it's just a bad idea, and you've wasted all the time you've spent learning it. The best thing to do when you've fooled someone, and he or she inevitably asks, "How'd you do that?" is to simply smile enigmatically. Not like a smart aleck, because the spectator will instantly dislike you, but smile in your most charming way—as if you'd really like to tell but just can't. And this is one of the greatest dangers in performing magic because it's too easy to fall into the trap of being disliked. Many people don't like to be fooled; they feel belittled.

They must like you.

You must charm them.

And you must practice each trick about one hundred times, often in front of a mirror, until you can do it without hesitation and without worrying about where your fingers go or what to say. Until you can learn to perform a trick without guilt. This is vital, because when you perform magic your goal is to concentrate on the audience and project your personality as David Berglas suggests, **not** to look down at your hands with concern.

And with that, which sounds so simple but takes many magicians a lifetime of experience to understand and master, I will send you on your way to a world of mystery and fun. Remember those two words, because they embody everything that is wonderful about magic.

Richard Kaufman

FOUR KINGS FOUND

Here's a surprising start to learning magic—it's easy to perform a miracle

Let's start with something simple—a trick that doesn't require you to do anything but set up a few cards in advance, then give instructions to the spectator. The great thing about this trick is that the very act of dealing psychologically misdirects the audience. In other words, what they do leads their thoughts in a direction other than the actual method.

Set up a deck as follows, from the top down (all cards face down): Four indifferent cards, four kings, four aces. The rest of the deck.

Step 1

- With the deck held face-down, explain that you are going to demonstrate what you would like the spectator to do in a moment as you begin to deal cards alternately into two piles side by side on the table (left, right, left, right, for example).

- Deal two cards into each pile, then gather those four cards and put them on the **bottom** of the deck. (You have eliminated the four indifferent cards from play, and the kings are now on top of the deck.)

Step 2

This is your view of the spectator's hands—the photo is not upside down!

- Hand the deck to the spectator and say, *"Begin dealing cards into two piles as I did."*

- Count silently; after at least eight cards have been dealt (the kings and aces), say, *"Feel free to stop at any point."*

- When the spectator stops dealing, say, *"Are you satis-*

fied? You can drop a few more down or take a few away."

- Either way, the aces and kings—the only cards you care about—are already on the table.

- Place the rest of the deck aside.

KNACK MAGIC TRICKS

Step 3

- Square the two piles. Gesture toward one of the piles and ask the spectator to divide it into two packets, following the established dealing procedure. In other words, he is to create two piles by dealing the cards alternately from one to the other.

- When that's completed, have the spectator divide the second large pile into two smaller packets in the same way, by dealing. That will leave four packets of about equal size.

Make a big deal out of letting the spectator turn over the cards—he feels like he's doing the magic.

Step 4

- There is a king on top of each pile with an ace beneath it. Slowly turn over the top card of each packet to reveal the kings, dealing them to the table in front of the piles.

- Allow time for the spectator to enjoy what just happened. Continue, *"Your turn. Snap your fingers once over each packet, then turn over the top card of each one."* When the spectator follows your instructions, he'll be astonished to turn over the four aces.

1

NINE CARDS

This amazing interactive trick can be done anytime, anywhere— even over the phone

(Created by Jim Steinmeyer)

This automatic trick is a work of genius—you can do it in person, with your back turned, while you are out of the room, over the telephone, by recording your voice and playing it back for the spectator, even by embedding the instructions as an audio or video file on your Web site. Almost all the instructions are in the form of a script. The photos show everything from your view as you are watching the spectator follow your instructions. It couldn't be easier as long as you memorize what you're supposed to say.

All you need is a deck of cards, which can be borrowed.

Step 1

- Say, *"For this next trick I need you to actually help me. It's important that you have a deck of cards. Please mix them up and then take nine cards out of the deck. It doesn't matter what cards you select, just nine cards at random. No jokers."*

- The spectator takes nine cards out of the deck and deals them into a pile on the table.

Step 2

The spectator remembers the seven of spades in this example.

- Say, *"Good. You're sure that there are just nine? You can put the rest of the deck aside. We won't be using it. I'd like you to square up the nine cards and hold them face down in your hands. I need you to select one of those cards. Since I don't have any idea what they are, here's how we'll do it. Turn the cards toward you and fan them out, just like a hand of cards. Good. I want you to remember the third card from the back of the fan; that is, the third card from the top of the packet, not from the face. Don't take it out, just remember it."*

2

Jim Steinmeyer is one of the most remarkable men in magic, but you've probably never heard of him. That's because he works behind the scenes, developing the illusions you've seen performed by many magicians, including Doug Henning, Orson Welles, and even David Copperfield (for whom he created the Vanishing Statue of Liberty). Jim has created over one hundred illusions, and every day magicians are performing them all around the world. He also creates close-up magic, and Nine Cards is one of his most famous tricks—David Copperfield used it on one of his TV specials. Jim is also a prolific author and biographer, writing about the history of magic in books such as *Hiding the Elephant* and *Glorious Deception* (a biography of Chung Ling Soo).

Step 3

The spectator spells "S-E-V-E-N" and deals five cards to the table.

- Now say, *"Square the cards and turn them face down again. I want you to mix the cards, but we're going to do it in a special way, depending upon the name of the card you selected. Let me explain first. If you picked an ace, for example, you'd deal cards face down onto the table, one on top of another, spell-* ing that name: 'A-C-E' If you picked a seven, you'd spell 'S-E-V-E-N,' or jack, queen, king."

- Continue: *"Do that now. Spell the value of the card, dealing one card on top of another."*

Step 4

- Now say, *"There are some cards on the table in front of you and some still in your hands, right? Take those cards in your hand and drop them on top of the cards on the table."*

NINE CARDS (continued)

Just because there's nothing for you to do physically during this trick doesn't mean there's nothing for to do. You must memorize the script in advance, but there are no secret moves for you to worry about because the trick works itself.

This allows you to spend your time doing the most important thing of all: giving the trick a great presentation where your personality and charm really shine. You can practice this by recording yourself performing the trick, saying your lines,

Step 5

- Continue: *"Now, pick up the whole packet again. Since the middle name of every card is 'of,' we need to spell 'O-F.' Do it just as you did before, dealing one card on top of the other. Take the cards in your hand, drop them on top, and pick up the whole packet."*

Step 6

In this case the spectator would spell "S-P-A-D-E-S."

- Say, *"The last name of your card will be either 'clubs,' 'hearts,' 'spades,' or 'diamonds.' I want you to spell that. If you picked clubs, spell 'C-L-U-B-S,' one on top of another. Do that now. Whatever cards are in your hand, drop them on top of the ones on the table."*

then listening to it. It will make you cringe at first, but there's no better way to learn how to change what you're doing than listening to it, or seeing it, yourself. Don't hesitate to be critical of yourself—if you don't like what you see or hear when you watch yourself perform, change it!

• • • • VARIATION • • • •

There are many ways to end this trick—if you're sitting there with the spectator, you could also have the cards dealt face up to the table in a row and ask the spectator to wave his hand over them while you hold his wrist. Suddenly push his hand down onto his card (the fifth card dealt).

The spectator never sees what is shown here—this is just to show you where the chosen card is at this moment.

Step 7

- Continue: *"Now, you have to admit that there's no way that I know what card you picked. And, because of that, I have no way of knowing how you mixed them up, since the way you mixed them depended on the number of letters: Two is different than queen, clubs is different than diamonds. So,* *I can't know where your card ended up."*

- That's a fib. One of the fun things about performing magic is that it gives you license to lie at will. The selected card is dead in the middle of the packet: fifth from the top or bottom. The photo is an exposed view.

Step 8

- The simplest and perhaps most mysterious way to end this trick is to have the spectator call out the names of the cards one at a time as he deals them off the top of the packet.

- When he says the name of the fifth card, yell, *"STOP!"* Say it loudly for dramatic effect, then add, *"That is your card."*

5

NUMEROLOGY
Card tricks play into people's fascination with numbers

(Created by Larry Jennings)

A card seemingly remembered at random is magically located at the thirty-second position from the top, the spectator's lucky number. Like the other self-working card tricks in this chapter, other than arranging a few cards on top of the deck before you start, you're free to concentrate on your presentation.

This trick, incidentally, works on a clever adaptation of an ancient mathematical principle. People have been using mathematics in card tricks since at least 1593, when the first

Step 1

- In advance, secretly transfer four cards (a ten, nine, seven, and six of any suit) to the top of the deck.
- Remove the jokers from the deck—this can either be done ahead of time or openly as you start the trick.

Step 2

Note how the cards from the right-hand half, the original top cards, fall last.

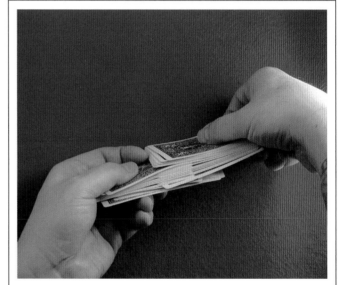

- Perform a riffle shuffle that does not disturb the four cards on top of the deck. Simply allow the original top four cards to fall last.
- Say, *"Have you ever thought about the way numbers seem to pop up in our lives again and again? There are people who believe in a science called 'numerology,' which posits that numbers can predict the future."*

mathematical card trick was published in a book by the Italian Horatio Galasso. The danger in using mathematics is that the mechanics become obvious—you don't want it to be apparent to the spectators that a simple self-working principle is what's causing the magic to occur. So, the best mathematical tricks are those that utterly disguise the underlying method so you get the credit.

Step 3

Gesture with your finger as you ask the spectator to cut the packets, helping to clarify what you want him to do.

- Ask a spectator to assist you as you place the deck face down on the table. Instruct him to cut the deck into four piles that each have about the same number of cards.

- Say, *"First cut the deck in half, then cut each of those halves in half."*

Step 4

Keep track of where the top of the deck is during the cutting process.

- You're going to force the original top quarter of the deck, which has the four set-up cards on top. Ask the spectator to point to two packets. *"Indicate two of the packets."* There are only two possibilities: Either the top quarter is included in the two he selects, or it isn't.

NUMEROLOGY (continued)

A simple verbal technique will be taught here—something that allows you to eliminate lots of sleight of hand. With it, you can force the spectator to select the particular thing you want—a quarter of the deck, in this case. The common names for this technique are "magician's choice" or *equivoque*

(ek-wuh-voke). It's a verbal control that is simple to do, provided you say things with conviction and, no matter what choice the spectator makes, you respond as if you were always going to say the same thing—even though what you say changes based upon his choices. This is the secret of

Step 5

The original top quarter of the deck is on the right here.

- If the packet with the original top four cards was *not* one of the ones chosen, then reassemble the two chosen packets and take them into dealing position in your left hand.

- If the top quarter *is* among the two he's chosen, then push those two packets forward slightly and pick up the other two.

- Either way, the result is the same: **The original top portion of the deck remains on the table.**

Step 6

- Next, ask him to indicate one of the two packets remaining on the table.

- If he indicates the top quarter, push it forward, then pick up the other packet, adding it to the cards already in your left hand.

- If he indicates the other packet, then pick it up and add it to the cards in your left hand. Either way, the result is the same, and you end up pointing to the original top quarter of the deck alone on the table.

magician's choice and the reason behind its title: While the spectator thinks he's controlling things and making choices, you are actually controlling things and making him pick the things you want (without him knowing it, of course). In this case, you are forcing the spectator to pick a particular packet of cards. Never use words like *pick*, *select*, or *choose*. Use neutral terms such as *indicate* or *point*.

Step 7

Demonstrate by dealing two or three cards quietly off the top of your cards face down to the table in a pile one at a time.

- Ask the spectator to count the number of cards in the packet that remains. *"Now I did not force you to cut the deck at any particular spot, is that correct?"* "Yes."

- *"And I did not force you to point to any particular packet on the table, is that correct?"* "Yes."

- *"Good. Now I'll turn away, and I want you to very quietly count the number of cards in that packet that remains. Do it like this, and please remember the number."*

Step 8

Don't give the spectator any cause to think you're peeking when you turn away. You can even hold your hand by the side of your face to emphasize that your vision is blocked.

- Pick up the cards you just dealt and return them to the top of your packet.

- Turn away and let the spectator count the number of cards in his packet.

- Ask if he's finished, then face him. *"Now you have to agree that's a random number. I mean, that packet could have had another number of cards in it if you cut the deck differently, is that correct?"* "Yes."

NUMEROLOGY (continued)

Tricks where cards are dealt to the table are made entertaining by your personality and presentation.

The vital point in any card trick where a card is chosen is to make sure the spectator remembers it! You'd be amazed how often people forget the card they've chosen. So, when you reach his number, give him time and strongly emphasize how important it is that he remembers the card. Some magicians even humorously say, *"Please remember your card; otherwise, the end of the trick just isn't very exciting!"*

The fact that you make a joke emphasizes the need to remember the card in a humorous way.

You can also ask the spectator to alert one of his friends to also note the card he's remembering, ensuring that at least one of them will remember it.

Step 9

- Ask the spectator to remember the card at his number. *"I'll deal cards face up onto the table and look away. I want you to remember the card that happens to fall at your random number."*

- Turn your head away and begin dealing off the top of your packet, turning the cards face up as you lay them on the table. Deal exactly twenty cards in a horizontal row from right to left (keeping the indices right side up for the spectator). *"Are you remembering the card at your random number?"*

Step 10

- Using your right hand, scoop up the twenty cards without disturbing their order, square them, and turn them face down. Leave them on the table.

- Place the cards that remain in your left hand on top of the tabled packet you just scooped up—the spectator's counted packet remains as is on the table.

10

Larry Jennings was a great bear of a man who loved nothing more in life than to perform card tricks for people at The Magic Castle in Hollywood, California. You would often find him sitting in the main bar, doing the kinds of miracles that most magicians can only dream of. It seems paradoxical that he was a plumber and boiler repairman during the day—his enormous hands moved as gently as a butterfly's wings. He had a huge repertoire and could often perform fifty tricks in one sitting.

Today he is remembered as one of the greatest close-up magicians of the late 20th century.

This miming action is important so the spectator understands that he is to deal out cards as if dealing hands in a poker game.

Step 11

- Demonstrate (mime because you're not holding any cards) dealing four cards off the top onto the table in a row as you say, *"So far, random numbers have played a very important part in this trick. But we're not finished yet. You still have a packet of cards. Please deal it into four smaller packets on the table, as if you were playing poker, like this."*

- Continue with another one or two cards, so the spectator understands that he is to deal the cards in a regular manner.

- Say, *"Please turn over the card on top of each little pile."*

Step 12

- *"They appear to be ordinary cards, just random numbers . . . let's add them together. Ten and six equals sixteen, plus nine equals twenty-five, plus seven equals thirty-two. That's your lucky number."*

- Pick up the large portion of the face down deck and hand it to him. Ask him to count down to the thirty-second card.

- Say, *"Please count down to your lucky thirty-two, and let's see how the numbers have influenced your life today."* When he turns over the thirty-second card he will discover his chosen card.

MIX IT UP!

Tear it, spell it, match it—do the impossible with five cards

(Created by Paul Curry)

Five cards are randomly chosen from a deck by a member of the audience. The magician tears the five cards in half. No matter how often the spectator asks the performer to mix the halves, the matching halves of each card always find each other. This is an impossible-looking effect: It seems that the spectator is given enormous leeway and so many choices that the end result is genuinely amazing.

Step 1

- You need an old deck of playing cards that you can destroy. Give the deck to a spectator and ask her to remove any five cards. Once done, place the rest of the deck aside—it won't be used again.

- Hold all five cards square and face down. Tear them in half widthwise. Your right hand places the half-cards it holds on the table to your right.

Step 2

Make sure you don't just put the whole left-hand packet down at once! You must count the cards to the table one at a time.

- Deal the half-cards that remain in your left hand onto the table into a pile one at a time, secretly reversing their order.

- This second pile should be to the left of the first one.

WHO INVENTED THIS?

Paul Curry invented what is perhaps the most famous card trick of the twentieth century, Out of This World, in which the spectator is seemingly able to separate all the red cards from the black cards without looking at the faces. While Curry performed difficult sleight of hand, he also excelled in creating magic that is deceptively simple, such as this effect. He wrote *Magician's Magic* in 1965, an excellent book for the public on both the performance and history of magic.

Step 3

Point to the packets one at a time to emphasize the spectator's free choice.

- To the spectator who first selected the five cards, say, *"We're going to play a little game called 'Will the Cards Match?' I am going to spell out each of the words in the phrase 'Will the Cards Match?' and at any time you may tell me to switch packets—right in the middle of spelling the word! In fact,* *it's more amazing the more often you ask me to switch. Also, at the beginning of each word, you tell me which packet to start spelling with."*

Step 4

- Ask her to point to either packet—you pick up the one she indicates. Begin to spell "W-I-L-L." For each letter, openly transfer the top card to the bottom of the packet.

- Make sure she understands that she can tell you to switch packets at any time. If she does, put down the packet you're holding and pick up the other one.

MIX IT UP! (continued)

The apparently random nature of the spectator's choices seems important, but is actually irrelevant! It's hard to believe, but no matter how many times the spectator tells you to switch packets, it makes absolutely no difference whatsoever in the outcome—the end result is predetermined by the number of letters in the words that are being spelled. You can even substitute other words if you like, as long as the number of letters is the same.

Step 5

- Then continue to spell the word, beginning with the letter after the one she stopped you on in the other packet. In other words, if she stopped you after *"W-I,"* then you would resume spelling in the other packet by saying *"L-L."* Remember to transfer a card from top to bottom for each letter.

It does not matter if she never tells you to switch or asks you to switch packets on every letter. After you've finished spelling, place the packet on the table.

Step 6

You're going to form two vertical rows of half-cards.

- Take the top half-cards off of both packets and place them together in a separate spot on the table, away from the packets.

•••••••••••••••••• RED ● LIGHT •••••••••••••••••

It's easy to get messed up here if you don't pay close attention to your spelling, particularly if the spectator is asking you to move from packet to packet, often in the middle of spelling a single word. So go slowly! Not only will this help to keep things clear for the audience, but it will also prevent you from making mistakes.

The top card from each packet after you've spelled "T-H-E" is placed onto the table in a new spot.

Step 7

- Repeat it again, this time spelling *"T-H-E."* Then place a second pair of half-cards onto the table.

- Repeat it again, this time spelling *"C-A-R-D-S."* Then place a third pair of half-cards onto the table.

- Repeat it again, this time spelling *"M-A-T-C-H."* Then place the fourth pair of half-cards onto the table.

Step 8

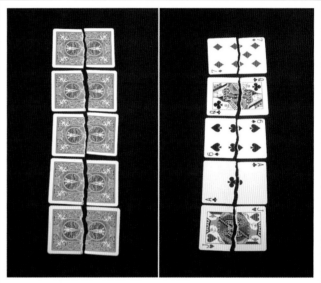

- You will be left with a single half-card from each packet—pair these together on the table.

- Say, *"Do the cards match . . . of course!"* Turn over the pairs of half-cards one at a time to reveal that all the halves have found their proper matching mates.

DON'T TOUCH THE CARDS

It's a genuine miracle when the spectator controls his own card without knowing it

(Created by Jack Miller)

The magician explains that he will show the audience a card trick in which he will never touch the deck. He asks anyone from the audience to assist him by cutting the deck anywhere and looking at the card he has cut to. The deck is then cut many times by the volunteer, both face down and face up. The magician announces that the chosen card is now, for example, ten cards down from the top of the deck. When the volunteer counts down to the tenth card he finds his selected card.

Step 1

- Before you begin, set the ace, two, three, four, five, six, seven, eight, nine, and ten of clubs in numerical order while they are face up with the ace at the face of the packet and the ten at the back.

- Place those ten set-up cards on the face of the deck.

Step 2

- Begin by setting the deck on the table face down and saying, *"I will not touch the deck during this amazing feat."* Ask for a volunteer.

- The photo shown here may look silly to you—why would I have a picture of a deck sitting alone on the table? Because that's what the audience will remember: an isolated deck on the table that you never touched.

Jack Miller was a professional magician who lived in New York City in the mid-twentieth century. He was a "character," doing magic with the air of an old Yiddish vaudevillian. He was one of the first magicians to create a truly unique and original version of the Linking Rings. I wish I could tell you about his greatest creation, but because it's an invisible gimmick that a lot of magicians still use I'll have to "hold out" on you.

Step 3

Make sure the person cuts the deck only once—in half and not into three or four piles.

- Say, *"Cut the deck once and place the part you've cut off onto the table next to the half that remains."*

Step 4

The spectator would not normally turn the card over this far because he doesn't want you to see it—it's shown that way in this photo only for clarity.

- When he has done that, continue, *"Please look at the top card of the lower half of the deck, that's the spot in the center that you cut to. Do not let me see the card, but you can show it to everyone else if you like."* Once you've seen that he's following directions, you can turn your head away so he feels free to show the card to other spectators (if there are any).

DON'T TOUCH THE CARDS (continued)

Resist the urge to touch the deck during this trick! That will make you nervous at first, but the entire point is that the spectator does every single thing from first to last. This gives the trick its utterly impossible flavor and is why it's a favorite of professional magicians around the world. The only danger in performing this trick is that the spectator will cut the deck into three piles, rather than only two, at some point. So, it's up to you, by using clear patter and gestures and being somewhat forceful in your instructions, to ensure that no mistakes are made.

The simplest way to do this is by using your first finger to point from the top of the deck to the table—where the cut-off half should be placed. Then point to the original bottom half and indicate it should be placed on top.

Step 5

- Say, *"Place your card, face down, on top of the half that you cut off. Now place the entire lower half of the deck on top of it, burying your card in the center. You may now cut the cards a few times if you like."* Here you must gesture that the volunteer is to give the deck "straight" cuts—that is, cut off half, then put the other half on top.

Step 6

- Say, *"Please turn the deck face up."* Casually (but immediately) look for any of the ten club cards you set on the bottom of the deck. At any time you may see one of those club cards on the face of the deck. For example, when he turns the deck face up you might see the four of clubs on the face (as in the photograph).

- You immediately know that his selected card is fourth from the top when the cards are face down. If you see the five of clubs, then his card is fifth from the top, and so on.

Harry Houdini's Water Torture Cell Escape was performed in a glass water tank and designed to thrill his audiences. His ankles were locked in heavy wooden stocks, then the escape artist was lowered into the water, and the stocks were locked to the top of the tank. A curtain was pulled around the tank to conceal Houdini. After a minute or two, Houdini emerged, dripping wet. The curtain was pulled away to reveal that the stocks and tank were still locked securely. The 1953 Hollywood film about Houdini starring Tony Curtis (himself an amateur magician) portrayed him as dying in the Water Torture Cell. He actually performed it hundreds of times for over thirteen years and never failed to escape.

Step 7

- So, if he turns the deck face up, and you see the four of clubs, ask him to turn the deck face down again. Close your eyes for a moment and concentrate, then announce that his card is fourth from the top.

- Ask him to count cards off the top of the deck, one at a time, placing them off to one side face down. When he reaches the fourth card (in our example), ask him to name his card, then turn over the card he is holding. It will be the same one.

Step 8

- Let's say, however, that you do not see one of the club cards when he turns the deck face up. Ask him to cut the face up deck. There's a chance he may cut into the ten club cards the first time. If not, ask him to complete the cut, then cut the deck again.

- Keep asking him to cut the deck again until he cuts into the run of club cards. Then, have him turn the deck face down and count down to whatever number club card you saw on the face. The card at that number will always be the one he picked.

MY UNCLE CHEATED AT CARDS

Every magician needs to be able to make it appear as if he or she can cheat at cards

(Created by Edward Marlo, Martin Gardner, and Harry Lorayne) The phenomenal popularity of poker means that, if you do card tricks, you will often be asked if you can cheat at cards. Here is the perfect demonstration that makes it appear as if you have tremendous ability at card cheating, when, in fact, this requires no sleight of hand at all. During the course of a cheating demonstration, you automatically set up a climax that gives you a poker hand that can't be beat.

Step 1

Borrow a deck of cards for this if you can perform the following set-up without getting nervous.

- Take the deck and hold it with the faces toward you. Say, *"When I was a boy my uncle taught me how to cheat at cards. The first thing you need to do is find the four aces."* Spread through the cards (with the faces held toward you) and slip the four aces to the face of the deck one at a time as you come to them. This is an open action—you're merely doing what you said.

- Also, at the same time, slip the ten, jack, queen, and king of spades to the rear of the deck. Note that the ace of spades should be on the face of the deck.

Step 2

You can also just set the four spade picture cards on top of the deck in advance, making the trick even simpler.

- In order to both set up the spade flush and find the aces at the same time, you need to be able to speak to the audience in a dynamic and interesting way to provide misdirection. The fact that you're looking for the aces is not a secret, but the gathering of the spade flush cards needs to go unnoticed. (If that's too difficult, then you have the option of setting up all the cards in advance, flush on top, aces on bottom, and bringing out the stacked deck to start the trick.)

Step 3

- Holding the deck face up, spread the bottom four cards to display the four aces (remember that the spade must be at the face).

- Say, *"My uncle did some very sneaky things."*

Step 4

- Square the deck and turn it face down, holding it in dealing position in your left hand. Deal a five-handed round of poker, dealing the first card to a spectator and the last card to yourself. However, you openly take the card for your hand from the bottom of the deck as you say, *"He used to deal his own cards from the bottom—I've never been able to make it look very good."* There's not supposed to be anything deceptive about this because it's a demonstration: You just stick your fingers under the inner end of the deck and openly draw the card out.

MY UNCLE CHEATED AT CARDS (continued)

Of all the card-cheating routines that magicians perform, this one is by far the simplest. That's because it's automatic: The initial part, where you openly pull the aces out from under the deck while dealing the first round of poker hands, sets up the second part by spreading out the cards for the royal-flush ending into the required positions—every fifth card. So, when you deal the second round of poker hands, the royal-flush cards are deposited into your hand with no sleight of hand required. The real method behind this trick is mathematical, yet it's so cleverly disguised that even most magicians don't realize it.

No matter how obviously you pull the aces from the bottom of the deck, there are still some spectators who will be surprised that they're in your hand.

Step 5

- Repeat the deal four more times so each poker hand ends up with five cards in it.

- Deal rather quickly to the first four hands, then deal your card from the bottom very slowly each time.

Step 6

- Turn over your poker hand to display that it contains four aces and one other card.

- Then pick it up, turn it face down, and drop it on top of the balance of the cards in your left hand.

- Your right hand next gathers the remaining four hands (which have remained face down), dropping them one on top of the other and eventually dropping the whole thing on top of the deck.

Another way to perform this trick is to secretly switch in the deck with the four spade flush cards already on top. You will find The Joker Deck Switch explained on page 35, and it allows you to secretly switch decks with no sleight of hand.

ZOOM

Thinking that the royal flush in spades is of greater value than a royal flush in hearts, clubs, or diamonds is a common misconception. All have equal value in a poker game and trump all other hands.

Step 7

- Say, *"But I practiced and practiced, and now you'll never see me deal from the bottom."* Again deal a five-handed round of poker, dealing five cards to each player—the last card of each round goes to you. There's no fake-bottom deal here—everything comes cleanly off the top.

When you deal the cards for your hand off the top of the deck, do it very slowly so there's no doubt they're coming from the top this time.

Step 8

- After you've dealt the fifth card to your hand, say, *"Let's see what the other players have,"* as you turn the other four poker hands face up and spread them. At least one spectator is certain to notice that there is an ace in the second, third, or fourth hands. Wave off any comments and say, *"I've gradu-*

ated to the big leagues," as you turn your hand over and spread it to reveal a royal flush in spades: ace, ten, jack, queen, and king.

DO AS I DO

This classic of card magic involves two decks and puts the spectator into the center of the action

So far all of the tricks you've learned have been automatic: If you follow the instructions carefully, they will work themselves.

Now let's try the first trick where you have to do just a little more than that. Do As I Do is a classic card trick that still amazes.

The new thing you will learn here is called a "glimpse." The word is nothing new to you: You've "glimpsed" things many times. Here, however, it means taking a peek at something casually . . . nonchalantly, so no one notices.

Step 1

Step 2

The two of clubs is the card you must remember in this case.

- You need two decks of cards. Give one to the spectator and say, *"You have to do everything I do in order for our thoughts to meld."* Hold the deck in your right hand, with the faces to the left, and perform an overhand shuffle. Your left thumb peels cards or small groups off the face and allows them to fall onto the left fingers.

- After you've shuffled off a bunch of cards this way, place the cards that remain in your right hand on the face of those in your left hand and note the card on the face of the deck—this is called a "key card." Let's assume it's the two of clubs (although it could be any card depending upon when you stopped shuffling).

- Immediately turn the deck face down. The spectator will also have shuffled her cards—doing as you're doing.

Step 3

- Say, *"Now we exchange decks—you give me yours, and you take mine."*

- Do that, handing her your deck, face down.

Step 4

- Say, *"I'm going to look through your deck and choose a card—you do the same. Spread the cards with the faces toward you so I can't see them and pick out any card and remember it."*

- You spread through her deck and remove any card—its value is irrelevant because it will never be seen, so don't bother to remember it. Place it face down on the table. The spectator will do the same, removing a card from your deck.

DO AS I DO (continued)

The secret of this trick is the key card, an invaluable aid in performing card tricks. Although Do As I Do is an advanced use of the key card, you could use it for a simpler trick, to locate a chosen card, as follows.

Glimpse the card on the face of the deck using the overhand shuffle as described at the beginning of Do As I Do. Turn the deck face down and spread it between your hands. Ask a spectator to *"please select any card."* If the spectator tries to pick the bottom card, you will have a miracle because you already know what it is! But assuming she picks any other card, ask her to look at and remember it while you square the deck and put it on the table, face down. Ask the spectator to place her card face down on top of the deck and then give the deck a "straight cut." Say, *"Please make sure the cards are perfectly square."*

Step 5

- Now place the deck you hold face down on the table.

- Put the card you removed (the one you are supposedly remembering) on top of your deck, then cut your deck once (a straight cut: The top half is cut off, then the bottom half is placed atop it). The spectator will do the same thing.

Step 6

- Say, *"You're doing very well so far. Let's take back our original decks."* Give her back her original deck and take back the deck you started with.

- Continue: *"Look through your cards and remove the card you're remembering from the deck, then place it face down on the table. I'll do the same with the card I'm remembering."* She will spread through her deck, remove the card she saw in your deck, and place it on the table face down.

Pick up the deck, turn it face up, and spread it widely on the table so you can see the corner of every card. Don't bother looking for your key card yet—you don't want it to be obvious. Ask the spectator to extend one finger, then grasp her hand by the wrist and move her finger back and forth over the spread cards. This gives you plenty of opportunity to locate your key card. When you see it, lower her finger onto the card directly to its right—her chosen card.

ZOOM

It's okay to lie when doing magic tricks. In fact, the more convincingly you lie, the better your magic will be. Do As I Do is a good example of a trick that requires you to lie—but it only works if you don't feel guilty about it.

Step 7

- You, however, will do something considerably more sneaky. Your key card, the two of clubs, is directly above her remembered card in your deck. So, spread the deck with the faces toward you and look for the key card.

- When you spot it, the card directly to its right will be the card the spectator is remembering: the jack of diamonds in our example. Remove her card from your deck and place it face down on the table.

- Square the rest of your deck and place it aside.

Step 8

- Say, *"You appear to have done exactly the same things I did, but, of course, we couldn't possibly know what card the other is remembering. Yet, sometimes, when people work closely together, their minds form a sympathetic bond. On the count of three, let's both turn over our cards. One, two, three."*

- And when you both turn over your cards, you'll find that they're identical.

27

X-FORCE

"Forcing" a spectator to select a specific card allows you to do all sorts of remarkable tricks

(Created by Max Holden)

There are literally hundreds of ways for a magician to force a card on a spectator. This particular force is notable for its simplicity. In fact, it's so simple that you may doubt it will work. One of the most important lessons you'll learn in magic is that even the boldest strategy can be artfully concealed with a few simple words and something called "time misdirection." That means you do something, then talk for a moment or do something else before continuing. Even a shift in attention for a mere thirty seconds can help misdirect the audience.

Step 1

- Secretly look at the top card of the deck in a casual way. You might lower your hands beneath the edge of the table for a moment and take a look at it. Or you can simply spread the cards between your hands, facing you, and look at it. Let's assume the top card is the king of spades in this example. The spectator doesn't know what you're doing or why, and the trick hasn't started yet.

Step 2

- Afterward, place the deck face down on the table and wait a few moments before starting the force. Make some innocuous remark just to take the spectator's mind off the fact that the deck was in your hands a moment earlier.

- Say, *"Please cut the deck, as much or as little as you want, and place it here,"* as you point to a spot on the table close to the deck. Now the deck will be split into halves, and the card you are remembering is on top of the half that the spectator has just cut off.

Max Holden was the owner of a magic shop in New York City for many years. Magicians from all over the world came into his shop, not only to buy the latest books and tricks but also to meet other famous magicians. Aside from inventing this lovely sleight, he became notorious for helping Camel cigarettes to expose magic to the public in a series of magazine ads in 1933. The tagline, "It's Fun to Be Fooled, but It's More Fun to Know," caused a huge scandal in the magic community and would've promptly put Holden's shop out of business had his assistance become known. Holden managed to keep his involvement secret, and it was discovered after his death.

Use time misdirection before you lift off the top half, asking the spectator a question or telling a joke.

Step 3

- Pick up the original bottom half of the deck (the portion left behind by the spectator) and place it on top of the cut-off packet at an angle.

- The halves of the deck almost form an X.

Step 4

- Direct attention away from the deck for a moment by making some comments. Lift off the upper half of the deck with your right hand and indicate that the spectator should lift the top card of the lower half and look at it. Ask him to remember the card (and show it to everyone if other people are watching). Finally, ask the spectator to replace the card anywhere in the deck and shuffle the cards. You have successfully forced the original top card of the deck.

HINDU SHUFFLE FORCE
This oddly titled sleight involves a bit of sleight of hand to force a card

In the Far East some people shuffle cards a bit differently, but there's little evidence that the Hindu Shuffle comes from the Indian subcontinent (although a similar shuffle is common in Japan and other parts of Asia). Fortunately, no matter where it comes from, it's a genuine shuffle that also allows you to easily force a card.

Step 1

- Glimpse the bottom card of the deck as explained in Do As I Do at the beginning of this chapter using an overhand shuffle.

- Let's use the king of spades as our example as we did with the X-Force.

It's less awkward for your right hand to grasp the inner end of the deck if you rotate your left hand slightly counterclockwise at the wrist.

Step 2

- Afterward, place the deck face down in your left hand.

- Your right hand changes grips, grasping the inner end of the deck between the thumb, at the inner-left corner, and fingers, at the inner-right corner.

As to who invented the so-called Hindu Shuffle, it could have been a guy in Brooklyn in the early 1900s just as easily as someone in Asia. It's not a particularly natural way of handling cards, but many magicians use it because it's simple and can accomplish many things.

Step 3

- Your right hand lifts the deck about 1 inch so you can grasp the long sides of the top few cards between your left thumb, at the left long side, and left fingers, at the right long side. They pull off a small block of cards. Once the block clears, allow it to fall onto your left palm. Move your left palm

  under the deck while your left fingers move into position and pull off another block.

- When your hands separate, this second block of cards falls onto the first one already on your left palm. Do this repeatedly, and that's a Hindu Shuffle.

Step 4

After the spectator has seen the face of the card (you see only the back), drop the right-hand cards onto those in the left hand and give the deck to the spectator for a shuffle.

- In order to use it as a force, as your left hand pulls the first block off the top, say to the spectator, *"Please say 'Stop' at any time."* Continue to pull additional blocks of cards off the top of the deck until "Stop" is called. Then turn your right-hand palm toward the spectator and display the card on the

  bottom of its portion of the deck and say, *"Remember this card."* This, of course, is the original bottom card—it hasn't moved at all; however, the shuffling creates the illusion that cards are mixing.

31

COLOR-CHANGING DECK

Usually only professional magicians can perform a routine where the back of the whole deck changes color

(Created by Wayne Dobson)

England's master magician, Wayne Dobson, who suffers from multiple sclerosis, devised this routine because he has the use of only his left hand. If you have the use of both hands, that makes it remarkably simple to do. Here, the back of an entire deck of cards changes color except for the card chosen by the spectator. Although this type of trick is usually very complicated and often uses difficult sleight of hand, this version uses only a face up handling of the X-Force, which you learned earlier in this chapter.

Step 1

- You need two decks of cards with different-color backs—one red-backed, the other blue-backed.

- Remove any two blue-backed cards that are the same color and value, for example, the six of clubs and six of spades. Get rid of the rest of the blue-backed deck; you won't need it in this trick. Place both blue-backed cards on top of the red-backed deck.

Step 2

This is still part of the set-up—the spectators do not see you do any of this.

- Turn the deck face up and spread the cards at the rear: The first two are the black sixes. Count backward from the top six and remember the seventh card, your key card—the three of hearts in this example (you'll see a different card each time you do the trick).

- All you have to do is remember your key card. Square the deck, turn it face down, and insert it into the blue-backed deck's card box.

The supremely talented and funny Wayne Dobson was in his late thirties and a star of British television and Las Vegas when he developed multiple sclerosis. Since then he has continued to perform and helped destigmatize the notion of seeing a handicapped magician. He appears onstage in a wheelchair and has adapted the type of magic he performs to tricks that require mostly personality and presentation—both of which he has in abundance.

Step 3

- This trick starts with a silent psychological ploy: When you remove the deck from the blue card box, the audience will naturally assume the cards all have blue backs. You must not say anything about the backs. Just seeing the blue box and the blue back on the top card sends a strong silent message: BLUE. Place the card box aside.

Step 4 Here is where the trick really begins for the audience.

- Turn the deck face up and place it on the table, ready for a face up version of the X-Force described earlier in this chapter. Ask a spectator to cut off half the deck and place it on the table.

- You then lift the remaining portion of the deck and place it on top of his cut-off portion at an angle.

COLOR-CHANGING DECK (continued)

When you perform the X-Force with the deck face up, talk for a moment about coincidences and how often they occur in magic. Say, *"Do you believe in coincidence?"* If the spectator replies *"Yes,"* say, *"That's funny, so do I. What a coincidence!"* If he replies *"No,"* say, *"That's funny, neither do I. What a coincidence!"* This is what magicians call "time misdirection," which is helpful in making the X-Force deceptive. Note that your response differs based upon what he says, but this is not evident to the audience. Just like the verbal technique magician's choice, what you say must seem to be exactly what you would have said regardless of what the spectator's response was.

Step 5

- Say, *"Lets try for a magical coincidence with the card you cut to."* Lift off the upper half of the deck with your left hand. Point to the face up card on the face of the cards still on the table and say, *"We won't use this one since I can see it. Let's use the one we haven't seen."* Turn your left hand palm up

and use your left thumb to deal off the top face down blue-backed card. (The audience will see another blue back under it, helping to reinforce the illusion that this is a blue deck.)

- Turn your left hand palm down and replace its cards squarely on the tabled half.

Step 6

- The entire deck is once again face up with the second blue-backed card in the center.

- Lift the face up deck and spread the cards between your hands until you come to the key card (originally

seventh from the top—in our example, the three of hearts).

- Openly cut the deck so the three of hearts becomes the face card. Square the cards.

The Joker Deck Switch: Some tricks already explained require the deck to be set up. They are so strong that you want to close your performance with one; switching in the set-up deck makes this easier. The set-up deck, from which you have removed the Jokers, is in your pocket. Take the deck you are using first out of your pocket, remove the Jokers, and toss them on the table. Do your tricks. Then put the deck back in the box and replace it in your pocket. *Only then* do you notice that the Jokers are still on the table. Say, *"Oops, forgot about those;"* remove the set-up deck from your pocket. Hesitate, saying, *"Let me show you just one more."* Then perform your routine with the set-up deck.

Step 7

Deal off the next card, the six of spades, after "M-A-G-I-C" has been spelled.

- Hand the face up deck to the spectator and say, *"Since we're trying to create a magical coincidence, spell the word 'magic,' using one card for each letter and dealing the cards to the table."* Guide the spectator's spelling of *"M-A-G-I-C,"* making sure the cards remain face up.

- Take the balance of the deck from the spectator and deal the next card (after "C"), the blue-backed six, face up next to the first face down blue-backed selection.

- Lift the face up dealt pile from the table and place it onto the face of the deck.

Step 8

- Turn over the face down blue-backed selection to reveal the other black six—the mate to the six found by spelling "magic." Say, *"Look, that's quite a coincidence: Both cards are mates! Not only that, but they are both blue-backed."* Turn both cards face down to show the two backs—this won't mean anything until you say, *"Which is an amazing coincidence because the deck has red backs!"*

- Turn the deck face down and spread it widely on the table to reveal that all the backs are red.

35

THE DOUBLE LIFT
This basic sleight for advanced card magic is taught in a new way

Were this book devoted entirely to magic done with playing cards, the Double Lift would appear in many of the tricks. It is an essential tool for most card magicians. Succinctly, it is the lifting of two cards held together as one off the top of the deck. When the two cards are replaced onto the deck, the card that has been displayed is actually second from the top. The Double Lift is difficult to do well even for experienced magicians. I have, however, described an original simple method that is convincing and within your reach with a bit of practice.

One of the most important things to remember in lifting two cards as one is that a card is both light and flexible. Two cards are equally light and flexible. Your hand must remain relaxed while lifting the double card—it's not a heavy object.

Step 1

- Begin with the deck face down in dealing position in your left hand. Your left thumb spreads off the top card, which is taken by your right hand.

- While your right hand is gesturing with its card (as you talk), your left thumb gently slides the top card of the deck inward about ⅛ inch.

Step 2

- Your right hand places the card it holds squarely on top of the deck—the card your left thumb pushed inward will stick out from beneath it at the inner end.

- Lower your palm-down right hand over the deck, first finger curled lightly on top, second, third, and fourth fingers at the outer end, and thumb at the inner end—actually on the end of the protruding card.

To make a quick trick out of just a Double Lift, perform the sleight exactly as explained. You will end with a single card in your right hand and the card you've shown secretly on top of the deck in your left hand. Your right hand inserts its face down card into the center of the deck. Square the cards and snap your fingers. Now lift off the top card (exactly as you did the double card a moment earlier) and reveal that it has returned to the top of the deck. Magicians call this type of effect, where a card placed in the center rises to the top, the Ambitious Card.

Step 3

Step 4

- Now align the top two cards by lifting the inner end of the protruding second card slightly with your right thumb and shoving it forward. Your right thumb is now holding the elevated inner ends of the top two cards, which should be perfectly lined up.

- The next step is the nerve-wracking part when you first try it, but it's really not difficult at all. Your right hand simply turns palm up while holding the double card. Your first finger is pressing lightly against the center of the double card, buckling it to help keep things lined up.

- Stay in this position for about two seconds (counting *"one . . . two . . ."* in your head helps) before turning your right hand palm down and dropping (that's right—dropping) the double card back on top of the deck from a height of about 1 inch. Immediately spread off the top card with your left thumb and take it with your right hand; that's a Double Lift.

THE CHANGING CARD
It involves a chosen card, a mistaken discovery, and a miracle

Although at least one hundred years old, this is still one of the most effective card tricks you can perform. Its directness and simplicity have elevated it to classic status, and it is performed by the best magicians in the world every day. You can

do it, too. It falls into the category of classic tricks, such as the Linking Rings, Cut and Restored Rope, and Cups and Balls. These are tricks that have been performed (in some cases) for centuries because they embody perfection in magic.

Step 1

Normally you wouldn't see the two of clubs on the face of the right-hand packet when doing the Hindu Shuffle Force—we've exposed it solely for clarity.

- Begin as in step 2 of Do As I Do by doing a face up overhand shuffle and noting the card on the face of the deck after the shuffle. Then turn the deck face down.

- The card on the face of the deck, say the two of clubs just for our example (it could be any card), is your force card.

- Perform the Hindu Shuffle Force exactly as explained in chapter 3 to force the two of clubs on the spectator.

Step 2

- After the spectator has seen the card, slap the right-hand cards on top of those in your left hand, burying the force card. Immediately hand the deck to the spectator and ask her to shuffle it.

- Afterward, take the deck and spread it between your hands, faces toward you, and find the force card (two of clubs in this example). Say, *"I think I've found your card,"* and openly cut the deck, bringing the force card to the top. Square the deck and turn it face down.

Step 3

- Perform the Double Lift as just explained: Take the top card with your right hand and gesture with it while your left thumb slides the second card inward a tiny bit. As you gesture with the right hand's card, say, *"I think this is your card."* Return the card to the top of the deck and do the Double Lift, your right hand lifting the top two cards held as one—show the face to the spectator. Of course, it's not her card.

Step 4

If you perform this properly, the spectator will not even remember that the card rested atop the deck for a moment.

- Say, *"Double jumbo bummer!"* as you replace the double card, face down, on top of the deck. What you say may seem silly, but it often gets a chuckle, providing perfect psychological misdirection. Immediately deal off the top face down card and take it with your right hand.

- Say, *"A little magic might help: Please blow on it,"* as your right hand extends the face down card toward the spectator.

- After she blows on the card, slowly turn it face up to reveal the card she chose!

THE TRICK THAT FOOLED HOUDINI

Not many folks fooled the master, but Dai Vernon, the father of modern close-up magic, did

(Created by Dai Vernon)

Years ago Dai Vernon wrote, "[My] tag line, 'He fooled Houdini,' came about from my having fooled him in Chicago back in 1919. I fooled him six or eight times . . . I had him initial one card on the face and then turned it face down and very slowly placed it under the top card . . . making it now the second card down. And then I very slowly turned over the top card, and it was his initialed card, back on top. I did this over and over, and I remember Houdini kept saying, 'You must be using two cards,' but I kept pointing out the fact that he initialed the card and I would have had no way of duplicating it on a similar card."

Step 1

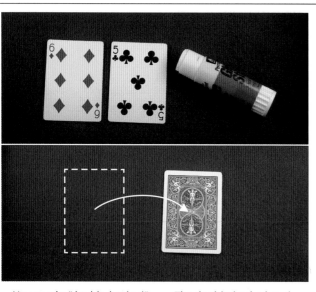

- You need a "double-backed" card. It's easy to make. Simply glue two cards face to face with a glue stick. Let them dry by placing them under some heavy books so the double-backed card is nice and flat.

- The double-backed card was created circa 1850 by Johan Hofzinser of Vienna, the creator of modern card magic. The double-backed card, whose back design must match that of the cards you're using, begins on top of the deck.

Step 2

- Spread the face down deck between your hands and allow a spectator to freely select any card. Once the card has been removed from the deck, ask the spectator to sign the face (it's wise to have a permanent marker available for this purpose—a regular pen or pencil won't write well on a playing card).

- Take the signed card with your right hand, holding it face up. Get ready for the Double Lift as already explained by sliding the top card of the deck slightly inward with your left thumb.

Dai Vernon was the father of modern magic, almost single-handedly creating much of the subtlety in sleights and tricks that you see magicians using today. He also lived long enough—to age ninety-eight—that he was able to see his students and the readers of his books take his thoughts and use them to create the backbone of modern conjuring. Canadian by birth, Vernon was reading difficult books on sleight of hand with cards before the age of ten. He was truly the master in our field. A multivolume definitive biography of this master, *Dai Vernon: A Biography*, has been written by Canadian magician and author David Ben.

Step 3

The blur in the photo shows how the card falls freely onto the deck.

Step 4

- Put the face up signed card on top of the deck. Continue with the Double Lift, your right thumb lifting the inner end of the second card and pushing it forward—your right hand will now be able to lift the top two cards perfectly squared as one.

- But do not turn your right hand palm up as before—here you simply move the double card all the way to the right until it's at the right side of the deck.

- Then, using your right hand, flip it over so it falls face down squarely on top of the deck.

- Spread off the top card and take it with your right hand. Then, your left thumb spreads over the new top card of the deck, and you openly slide the right-hand card (which the spectator assumes to be his signed card) under the deck's top card. Square the cards.

- Snap your fingers and turn over the top card to reveal that his signed card has risen to the top.

- This can be repeated three or four times, very slowly, so each successive "rise" is more mysterious than the one before.

CHICAGO OPENER

This classic trick is a favorite of professional magicians around the world

(Created by Frank Everhart and Frank Garcia)

A card is freely chosen and remembered by a spectator. It's returned to the deck, and the cards are cut. The magician spreads the deck and reveals that one of the cards has a different-colored back. That card is shown and, oddly enough, it's the very one chosen a moment earlier. The odd-backed card is placed aside, face down, and a second card is chosen. When the odd-backed card is turned over, it is now amazingly seen to match the second chosen card. This routine is another step up in your learning curve—it uses two sleights: the Double Lift and Hindu Shuffle Force.

Step 1

- You need one full deck of cards (let's assume it's blue-backed) and one card from another deck with a different-colored back.

- Let's assume that the odd-backed card you're going to use is a red-backed six of clubs. It could be any card, but we'll use the six of clubs just as an example for ease of understanding.

Step 2

The six of clubs with the red back goes on the face of the deck.

- Look through your blue-backed deck, locate the six of clubs, and place it on the face. Put the red-backed six of clubs on top of that.

- Square the deck, turn it face down, and you're ready to perform.

KNACK MAGIC TRICKS

42

WHO INVENTED THIS?

Frank Everhart was a master of "bar" magic, a subgenre of close-up magic that is performed by a bartender for his customers. It originated in Chicago but is now performed all over the world, even in Japan, where it has become a fad and where there are as many as fifty magic bars. Standing behind a bar when doing magic gives you, shall we say, certain "advantages." Frank Garcia, a New York magician, was a much-loved figure who wrote many books on close-up magic and appeared on TV many times. This is his version of the classic trick.

Step 3

- Begin the trick by spreading the face down deck between your hands and asking the spectator to select a card. Try to spread the cards widely so the spectator feels that she has a completely free choice— that's important.

- The outstretched fingers of both hands support the spread deck from beneath.

Step 4

- After she has removed the card, ask her to look at and remember it. While she's doing that, square the deck and place it face down on the table.

- After she has remembered her card, ask her to place it, face down, on top of the deck.

CHICAGO OPENER (continued)

Combining two of the sleights you've already learned in one trick is a great step forward in your ability to perform magic. Some difficult tricks require dozens of sleights performed in quick succession, so although it may seem intimidating to you at first to do two sleights in one trick, everything is relative.

The most important thing is that you don't worry about doing the sleights. Before you actually perform the trick, you must practice each sleight on its own many times until you have full confidence in your ability to do it without hesitation or guilt. Spectators can almost smell your fear, and, if they sense that you are nervous, they will become more vigilant and try to catch you rather than relaxing and enjoying your performance. Only when you can eliminate the feeling of guilt will you find it easy to incorporate them into the larger structure of a routine like Chicago Opener.

Step 5

Chosen card
Six of clubs red
Six of clubs blue

- Give the deck a straight cut: That is, cut off the top half and place it on the table, then complete the cut by placing the bottom half on top of it. You have openly buried her chosen card in the center of the deck. The photo shows the deck spread **only so you can see** the positions of the cards at this moment—the deck remains squared during the performance of the trick.

Step 6

- Say, in a conspiratorial tone, *"Before we started, I put a card from a different deck into this one. It's easy to spot."* Pick up the deck and spread it between your hands until the red-backed card is revealed in the center.

- Cut the deck at that point, place all the cards that were above the red-backed card beneath the portion of the deck in the left hand. The red-backed card is now on top.

Alexander Herrmann, billed as "Herrmann the Great," was America's favorite magician in the last decades of the nineteenth century. He was born in Paris, France, of a German-Jewish family. His father, Samuel, was a professional magician, as was his oldest brother, Compars. Alexander's specialty was delicate sleight of hand, which he performed with a light touch and accompanied by humorous, French-accented patter. He created our modern clichéd image of a magician: the tall, thin, devilish performer in a tailcoat who reaches into a hat and produces a rabbit. Herrmann looked like that and was one of few magicians who actually produced a rabbit from a hat.

HERRMANN

Step 7

- Ask, *"What was the name of the card you chose?"* At the same time, prepare for the Double Lift by taking the red-backed top card with your right hand and gesturing with it (keeping it face down). At the same time, your left thumb slides the top card of the deck inward a bit.

- Say, *"It would be pretty amazing if this card I put in the deck before the trick began was the one you picked, wouldn't it?"*

Step 8

- Replace the red-backed card on top of the deck, face down.

- Perform the Double Lift. This appears to show that the red-backed card is the card that the spectator chose. You actually are displaying the face of the chosen card but not its blue back (which is covered by the red-backed card).

CHICAGO OPENER (continued)

To remove any feelings of uncertainty you may have when performing a routine with several phases, such as this one, it will help to think of the trick like a small play. You must memorize the stage directions (the physical steps that must be performed in the proper sequence) as well as the script (the patter that you must speak at the proper times). Many magicians find it makes things easier to memorize the physical movements before the patter. However, once you have memorized both, you must always practice them together.

Learning to perform magic is no different than learning anything else: even something as simple as the alphabet. First you learn the letters, then you put them together to form words. Here you are learning movements and words, then putting them together to form tricks.

Dropping the double card onto the deck from the height of about 1 inch gives it a light look that subconsciously moves the spectators away from any thought that you might be holding more than one card.

Step 9

- Turn your right-hand palm down and drop the double card onto the top of the deck.

- Immediately deal off the top red-backed card, take it with your right hand, and place it face down on the table.

Step 10

- Say, *"I'd like you to pick a different card. Please say 'Stop,'"* as you begin the Hindu Shuffle Force described in chapter 3.

- Your right hand holds the deck at the inner end while your left thumb and fingers strip off small groups of cards from the top (which then fall onto the left palm).

Alexander was the stage name of vaudeville magician and mind reader Claude Conlin. His distinctive advertising was typical of the exotic trappings of his act; Alexander performed in a turban and silk robe, reminding his audience of Eastern mysticism and supernatural wonders. During his act, audience members would write questions and seal them in envelopes—they were encouraged to ask personal questions about their jobs or family. Alexander then picked up the sealed envelopes and, without opening them, divined each question. He then offered vague, "horoscope-like" bits of advice.

Step 11

Step 12

- When the spectator stops you, turn your right-hand palm up and display the six of clubs, which appears to be a freely chosen card. Use your left thumb to slide the six off the face of the right hand's cards and onto the table.

- Afterward, your right hand turns palm down and drops its part of the deck onto the cards in your left hand.

- There are two cards on the table: a face down red-backed card, which the spectator believes is the first card she picked, and a face up six of clubs. Place the deck aside.

- Lift one card with each hand and rub the face down red-backed card on the face up six of clubs. Say, *"The first part was just amazing, but this part is a miracle."* After a moment, turn the red-backed card face up to reveal a second six of clubs.

47

FOUR ACE REVERSO
Tricks in which cards magically turn over are always surprising

(Created by Shigeo Takagi)
Causing a deck of cards that's been mixed face up and face down to right itself is one of the most amazing tricks in card magic. Here, during the course of an overhand shuffle, the deck is turned various ways, face up cards being mixed among face down cards in a haphazard manner. It's a crazy kind of shuffle that the spectators will find quite curious. At

the end of the shuffle, the deck is spread to reveal that all the cards are facing one way with the exception of the aces, making a surprise appearance.

Most routines of this type involve a difficult false shuffle or some sleight that secretly reverses half the deck. Happily, this clever version does not.

Step 1

- Begin with the four aces secretly on top of the deck.

Step 2

- Flip the deck face up if it is not already, then grasp it in your right hand for an overhand shuffle.

- Shuffle cards into your left hand, your left thumb peeling off about a quarter of the deck as both single cards and small groups. Don't be too careful about this: Takagi never looked as if he was being too careful about anything.

WHO INVENTED THIS?

Shigeo Takagi was a monumental figure in Japanese magic. While his day job was at Japan's version of the Library of Congress, his real love was close-up and stand-up magic. He was responsible for bringing much of the knowledge of Western magicians to Japan through translating Western books into Japanese and lecturing on the subject to his compatriots. His forte in creating card magic was the ability to see simple ways to accomplish magic that usually required difficult techniques. I was pleased to write and publish an entire book on his creations, *The Amazing Miracles of Shigeo Takagi*, in 1990.

Step 3

Step 4

The inset photo shows the moment when the four aces are being shuffled onto the face up left-hand cards.

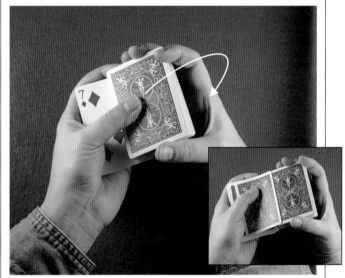

- Your right hand, holding three-quarters of the deck, turns palm down and rests its face down cards on the face up cards held by the left hand but spread halfway off to the right.

- Your left thumb moves onto the larger portion of the deck to hold it in place.

- Loosen the right hand's grip just enough so that you can turn it palm up, swinging it beneath the cards while still holding on. You'll find that your right hand is automatically holding the three-quarters of the deck in overhand shuffle grip.

- As you lift it, your left thumb begins the shuffle by peeling the first face down card off the deck and onto the face up cards.

- Rapidly shuffle/peel off another three face down cards onto the cards in your left hand. (Those four face down cards are the aces.)

ADV. CARD TRICKS

FOUR ACE REVERSO (continued)

Most tricks where a deck is seemingly mixed face up and face down (and then magically rights itself so the cards face all one way) require a false shuffle—making them difficult to do. The brilliant part of Shigeo Takagi's approach is that the shuffle is genuine. What creates the illusion is not only the turning over of the packets but also the raising of both hands

so the spectators can see the undersides of the cards during the portion of the shuffle described in the second paragraph of step 5 on this page. Even though it may seem obvious that you are merely showing the spectators the undersides of the cards, the visual impression created reinforces the face up/face down mix-up.

Step 5

- Without pausing, your left thumb moves beneath the left-hand packet and openly flips it over.

- At the same time, raise both hands and bend them back slightly at the wrists so the undersides of the cards are toward the spectators.

- Immediately shuffle another quarter of the deck on top of the cards in the left hand. This is done with the hands in raised position, which creates an odd illusion for the spectators of seeing more mixed-up faces and backs than actually exist.

Step 6

- Lower your hands back to normal position, your left thumb again openly flipping over the cards held in that hand. As soon as that half of the deck has completed its revolution, turn your right hand palm down and rest its face up cards partially on those in the left hand.

- Swing the right hand beneath, palm up. Your right hand will, once in that position, be grasping a face up packet in overhand shuffle grip.

A trick like this can seem confusing when you first read it because of all the changes in hand positions. Go slow! Look carefully at each photo both before and after you read the instructions beneath it. Take your time—this is not a cook-book. Often even experienced magicians must read and reread a trick description three or four times before they fully understand it. So, read the text, look at each photo, and try it slowly. You'll probably get lost at the point when you are supposed to raise your hands while doing the over-hand shuffle so the audience can see the underside of the deck. This is when practice in front of a mirror helps a lot—it will enable you to understand the illusion as seen by the audience. If you get lost, go back to the beginning and try it again ... SLOWLY.

Step 7

- Begin the shuffle, your left thumb pulling off the first face up card onto those in the left hand as the right hand pulls the packet away.

- Shuffle the balance of the cards from your right hand on top of the cards in your left hand. The aces have now been centered in the deck. This last shuffle, which involves half the deck, should be done in small groups so that it does not take inordinately longer than any of the prior shuffles.

Step 8

- Turn the deck face down and snap your fingers. Do a wide spread to reveal that all the cards are now face down with the exception of the aces, which are face up in the center of the deck.

QUADRUPLE COINCIDENCE

This trick packs a big wallop courtesy of clever ideas from two magicians

(Created by Mike Shelley)

The deck is shuffled, then given to the spectator, who is told to deal off a small packet of cards. The magician shuffles the deck again and allows the spectator to pick a card—it's the two of clubs. He spreads the deck on the table, face down,

to display its blue backs, then turns over the two of clubs to reveal that it's the only red-backed card in the pack. To prove that he knew the spectator would pick the two, the magician tells the spectator to turn over the packet he dealt at the beginning and look at the bottom card—it's also a two of

Step 1

- Let's assume you are going to use the two of clubs as your "force" card for this trick.

- You need a blue deck and its card box, a red-backed two of clubs, a 1-inch round sticker, and a pen.

Step 2

- You also need a "big" two of clubs. Although you can buy a "jumbo" deck of cards, you can also make the big card for this trick yourself. Cut out a piece of white cardboard that measures 7 x 4½ inches and draw the face of a two of clubs on it.

- Place this "big" two of clubs, face toward you, inside the inner breast pocket of your jacket or under you on the chair if you're not wearing a jacket.

clubs, and it has a sticker on it that reads, "I knew you would pick the two of clubs." To prove even more strongly that he knew the spectator would pick the two of clubs, he hands the card box to the spectator and asks him to read what's written inside the flap—"You will pick the two of clubs." And to prove unequivocally that the magician knew which card the spectator would pick, he pulls a jumbo card out of his pocket and tosses it to the table, revealing the two of clubs.

Step 3

- Set-up: Place the round sticker on the center of the face of the blue-backed two of clubs (which you've removed from the deck). Write "I knew you would pick the two of clubs" on it.

- Now place this card on top of the deck, face down.

Step 4

The photo shows the deck face up with the cards spread so you can see where everything is.

Blue-backed two of clubs   Deck   Red-backed two of clubs

- Set-up: Place the red-backed two of clubs on the bottom of the deck, face down.

53

QUADRUPLE COINCIDENCE (continued)

This is a real showpiece that famous magicians have used to close their close-up show. Larry Jennings, who was capable of doing the most difficult card tricks in the world, some involving twenty hard sleights in the span of a few minutes, chose this almost-self-working trick to end his shows at the famous Magic Castle in Hollywood. The lesson to be learned is, again, that it's the performance of the trick that is the most important part—the effect it has upon the audience is exponentially more important than the method. A simple trick well presented is much better than a difficult trick poorly presented.

Step 5

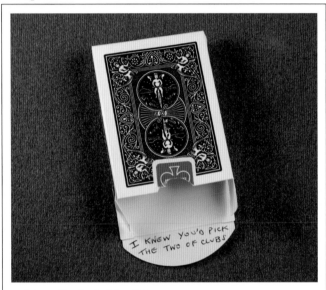

- Set-up: On the inside of the flap of the card box write, "I knew you'd pick the two of clubs."

Step 6

- Set-up: Place the deck inside the card box so that the face is against the side with the thumb notch.

- Place the case inside one of your pockets.

This trick, created by Florida magician Mike Shelley a decade ago, could easily be the highlight of any magical performance. Mike was introduced to magic at age eight by his father. He used to have a day job as a manufacturers' rep but gave that up to earn a living by performing, inventing magic tricks, and doing lectures. He's invented over 250 magic tricks and has been involved with both the IBM

(International Brotherhood of Magicians) and SAM (Society of American Magicians).

One of the great geniuses in our field, Larry Jennings, added a great script to Mike's trick that makes it both funny and more powerful. It is Jennings's script that is provided here.

Step 7

- Begin the performance by taking out the card box and holding it so the flap side is up (thumb-notch side down).

- Open the case and remove the face down deck. This handling keeps both the

card on the face of the deck and the writing inside the card box's flap from being seen.

- Place the partially open case off to your left.

Step 8

- Square the deck and say to the spectator, as you hand him the face down cards, *"Take the deck and deal cards onto the table in a pile one at a time until you feel like stopping."*

- Let him deal until he wants to stop, then extend your hand and take the balance of the deck.

QUADRUPLE COINCIDENCE (continued)

With these next few steps, the routine starts to gain a momentum toward unbelievable impossibility.

An important part of performing magic when you're using a table is geography. In other words, keeping everything on the table neat and in a spot where it doesn't visually interfere with the main point of focus. In this routine, a lot of cards,

a card box, and a jumbo card all end up in different places on the table. It can become a jumble if you're not careful—and there's a fine line between creating a jumble and putting things in specific spots (albeit close together) to create an overwhelming impression of impossibility.

Step 9

- Say, "*And I want you to say 'Stop,'*" as your right hand takes the bottom portion of the deck and you begin a Hindu Shuffle Force as explained in Chapter 3. Your left thumb and fingers pull groups of cards off the top of the deck, allowing them to fall onto your left palm.

- When the spectator stops you, turn your right hand palm up, revealing a two of clubs on the face of the packet. Say, "*Oh, look, you stopped me on the two of clubs.*"

Step 10

- Use your left thumb to peel the two of clubs off the packet and lay it on the table without allowing its back to be seen.

- Turn your right hand palm down and replace its cards, face down, on top of the cards still in your left hand.

- Say, "*Isn't it odd that you stopped me on the only red card in a blue deck?*" During that sentence, turn the deck face down and spread it widely across the table to display the blue backs.

- Then turn the face up two of clubs over to reveal its red back.

Harry Jansen (who later became famous under the stage name Dante) started his career as a vaudeville performer and a builder of magic apparatus for other magicians. This allowed him to become an expert at the secrets and techniques of magic, and his skills as a builder were highly regarded by his fellow professionals. This poster shows a wide range of Jansen's accomplishments. He appeared as a "transformist," changing costumes and characters with every illusion. The images include the production of a lady seated on a throne, a levitation and disappearance illusion, and the production of assistants from a small curtained cabinet.

Step 11

- Look at the spectators and hold both hands in the air, palms toward them, as you say, tongue-in-cheek, *"No, hold your applause."* Turn to the spectator and say, *"I know what you're thinking. You're thinking I used some incredible sleight of hand to cause you to stop on a red card in a blue deck, right?"* No matter how he responds, shake your head and say, *"I know that's what you're thinking."*

- Turn the red-backed card on the table face up and say, *"It was the two of clubs."* Leave it face up in the same spot on the table.

Step 12

- Point to the spectator's packet and say, *"Would you look at the bottom card of that packet you just dealt."* The spectator will either turn the whole packet over or pick it up and slide out the bottom card.

- Take the card with your right hand and hold it up for everyone to see as you say, *"Another two of clubs."*

- Pause a moment as you hand the card back to the spectator and say, *"It also has a sticker on it—would you read what the sticker says?"* The spectator reads, *"I knew you'd pick the two of clubs."*

QUADRUPLE COINCIDENCE (CONTINUED)

Here's your big finish—the moment when you've piled up so many unbelievable coincidences that the audience can barely breathe. First, the spectator stops you on the only red card in the blue deck. Second, that card turns out to match a chosen card, which, third, also has a sticker on it that states that you knew he would pick that card. Fourth, you've written the name of the chosen card in advance on the inside flap of the card box. And fifth, you pull an enormous duplicate of the chosen card out of your pocket. It's an avalanche of miracles.

Most of this routine is an exercise in presentation and acting. Aside from using the Hindu Shuffle Force at the beginning, all your attention should be devoted to charming the spectators and making them believe how impossible the unfolding

Step 13

- Then hold up your hands when the applause starts (and it will) and say, *"No, no . . . hold your applause because I know what you're thinking. You're thinking that through some incredible sleight of hand I made him stop on a red card in a blue deck, and then while he* *was looking at that I reached into my pocket* [point to your pocket] *and grabbed the sticker and put it on his card. But I really knew he was going to stop on the two of clubs."*

Step 14

- As you reach the end of that sentence, your left hand reaches over and picks up the card box. Hand it to the spectator and say, *"Look, I haven't been near this case since I opened it, have I? Would you read what it says inside the lid?"*

- The spectator reads, *"I knew you'd pick the two of clubs."*

events really are. Don't recite the patter with a snide or superior attitude—the script is funny not only because it's repetitious but also because it's outlandish. You couldn't possibly be doing the things you're saying, yet merely by saying them you're planting a seed in the mind of the audience that creates doubt. Doubt creates mystery. Mystery, combined with laughter and amazement, generates instant applause.

Step 15

- When the applause starts (and it will), immediately hold up your hands again and say, *"No, hold your applause, hold your applause. I know what you're thinking. You're thinking that through some incredible sleight of hand I made him stop on a red card in a blue deck, and then while he was looking at that I reached into my pocket and grabbed the sticker and put it on the card. And then while he was reading the sticker, I wrote that on the lid of the card box."* Pause for a second and sit back.

Step 16

- Continue: *"But I honestly knew he was going to stop on the two of clubs . . . otherwise* [reach into your breast pocket or under you and grasp the jumbo two of clubs], *why would I be carrying this darn thing around!"* Bring the jumbo card into view, its back toward the audience, and toss it face up on the table.

- Now accept your applause!

FIVE LITTLE PIGGIES
This is one of the few self-working coin tricks and a perfect start for the beginner

This trick is older than dirt—so old, in fact, that most people have forgotten about it. That's good for you because you have a fresh audience out there. The plot is simple and involves seven coins. Two of them are designated as wolves, the other five are piggies. You pick up one wolf coin and two piggy coins in each hand. A second later, when you open your hands, the two wolves are in one hand, and the five piggies are in the other. It's one of the few self-working coin tricks and, if presented properly, will surprise everyone. Make sure you don't leave out the patter; otherwise, it's just a transparent puzzle.

Step 1

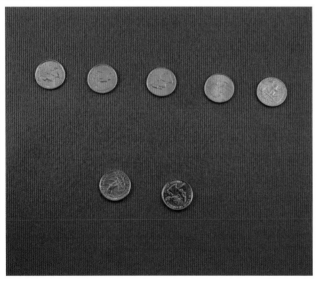

- You need seven quarters. Place them into two rows on the table: The outer row contains five coins, the inner row contains two. Say, *"You've heard about the three little pigs—this is a story about five piggies and two wolves."*

- Gesture toward the row of five coins when you mention the piggies, then toward the row of two coins when you mention the wolves. Because all the coins are identical, you have to work hard to keep the identities of the "wolves" and the "piggies" clear in the minds of the spectators.

Step 2

- Pick up the two coins in the inner row, one in each hand, and make a fist around them as you say, *"The wolves hide behind the bushes until no one is looking."*

Step 3

The photo is a stop-action view: Make sure to draw the coins completely inside your hands as you pick them up.

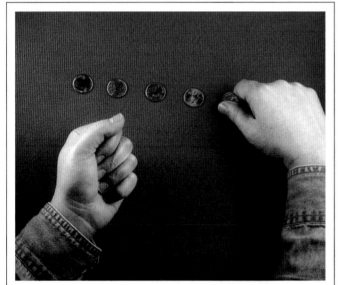

- Then say, *"After waiting a little while, when no one is around, the wolves sneak out and steal the piggies."*

- During the following sequence you must keep your hands closed loosely into fists so the spectators cannot see inside them.

- Your right hand picks up the first piggy using your right thumb to nip it against the side of your finger before drawing it completely inside the fist.

Step 4

Here is where you establish the rhythm that makes the trick deceptive.

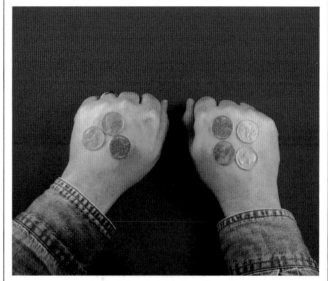

- Your left hand picks up the second piggy the same way, drawing it into the fist with your left thumb.

- Your right hand picks up the third piggy.

- Your left hand picks up the fourth piggy.

- Your right hand picks up the fifth piggy.

- You now have three coins in your left hand and four in your right. The photo allows you to see how many coins are contained in each closed fist—this is not visible to the audience.

FIVE LITTLE PIGGIES (continued)

Have you figured out how this works? Simple psychology covers the math. The spectators forget which hand you started with, and you need only to get a little bit ahead of them in order to create a miraculous result.

Of course, you don't have to call the coins "wolves" and "piggies." The more common parlance is "thieves" and "sheep," but the patter isn't as amusing. You can create virtually any patter story involving two distinct groups of characters and adapt it to this effect. For instance, "vampires" (or "zombies") and "victims." You could also use the theme of "jungle explorers" and "cannibals," or a particular duo of superheroes like Batman and Robin trying to catch five villains.

Step 5

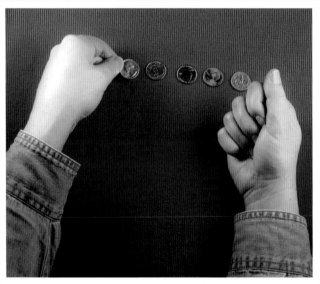

- Say, *"The wolves heard a noise and got scared, so they put the piggies back."* First, your left hand puts one of its coins (call it the first coin) back on the table.

- Then, your right hand puts a second coin back on the table.

- Your left hand puts a third coin back on the table.

- Your right hand puts a fourth coin back on the table.

- Your left hand puts a fifth coin back on the table.

Step 6

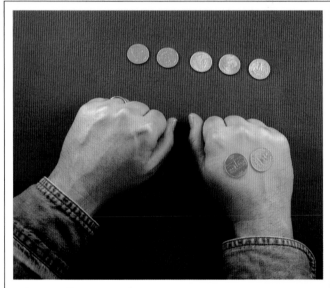

- You now have two coins in your right fist and no coins in your left fist. The spectators believe you still have one coin in each hand! Those little piggies are pretty clever.

Thomas Nelson Downs was an American vaudeville star. As a young man, he worked in the telegraph office in Marshalltown, Iowa, wiling his time by manipulating coins between his fingers. When he appeared as the King of Coins, his act consisted solely of sleight-of-hand magic, almost completely using stacks of half dollars that seemed to be juggled, flourished, or made to turn somersaults. His performances were enhanced with an engaging, droll personality. Downs's specialty was the Miser's Dream, in which he caught dozens of half dollars in the air, tossing each one into a tall silk hat.

Step 7

- Continue: *"After a minute or two went by, the wolves ran out and grabbed the piggies once again."*

- Your right hand picks up the first piggy.

- Your left hand picks up the second piggy.

- Your right hand picks up the third piggy.

- Your left hand picks up the fourth piggy.

- Your right hand picks up the fifth piggy.

Step 8

- Say, *"The wolves got very tired and fell asleep. When they woke up in the morning they were hungry . . . and disappointed to find that they were sleeping together."*

- Open your left hand to reveal only two coins. Conclude with *". . . and all the piggies were safe behind* the other bush,"* as you open your right hand to reveal five coins. The structure of this effect is clever enough that you may even fool yourself the first few times you try it.

A COIN VANISH

A simple, basic sleight that's easy to learn and allows you to do many things

To properly learn a sleight like this, you must practice the real action, then practice the false action so it looks as much as possible like the real action. In this case the real action is simple. Put a coin on the table and then lower your fingers over it. Drag it toward you and pick it up as it leaves the table edge. This vanish simulates that action.

Be certain to watch your right hand, supposedly the one containing the coin, as you raise it. Do not watch the coin fall into your lap!

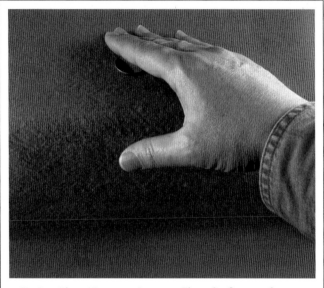

The coin can actually be farther away from the table edge, depending upon the particular trick in which you use this. It's easy to start with 3 inches.

Step 1

- Begin with a coin, any coin, on the table in front of you. It should be about 3 inches from the edge of the table.

- Place the fingers of your palm-down right hand flatly onto the coin. Your right thumb dips behind the edge of the table—this is a natural thing for your thumb to do.

Step 2

- Slide the coin inward until it falls off the edge and into your lap. Keep your right fingers together and straight as you do this.

- Watch the backs of your right fingers, not the coin falling into your lap!

It's imperative that you believe the coin to be in your hand—if you believe it, the audience will believe it.

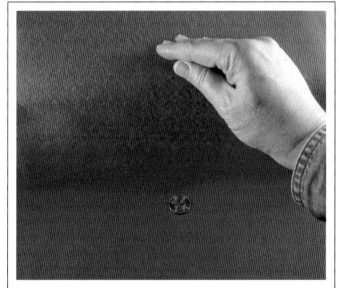

- Bring your right thumb up under your right fingers, as if to hold the coin there— this is what you would do if you were really picking up the coin.

Watch your right hand as you raise it with the coin supposedly inside your right fingers. Watching your hand will focus the attention of the audience on it (rather than giving them the opportunity to question where the coin might otherwise be).

- Now raise your hand, as if holding the coin, keeping your fingers together and straight with the thumb behind them.

- You can do various things to make the coin vanish, some of which we will explore in this book. For the moment, simply raise your right fingers to your mouth and blow on them (it is at this instant that the audience thinks the coin vanishes).

- Now turn your hand palm toward the audience and spread the thumb and fingers widely to reveal an empty hand.

QUARTER TO TEA

There's more hidden in a good bag of tea than merely dried leaves

Now that you have learned how to make a coin vanish, you can do a trick where the coin reappears in an "impossible" location. This is a trick that requires you to alter a normal tea bag in advance. Once the tea bag is prepared, you can perform the trick in someone's home or in a restaurant—both of these are what magicians call an "informal" situation, that is, where you're just sitting around with some friends and you casually do a trick during the course of conversation. A "formal" situation is where you are sitting in front of everyone who knows there's going to be a show.

Step 1

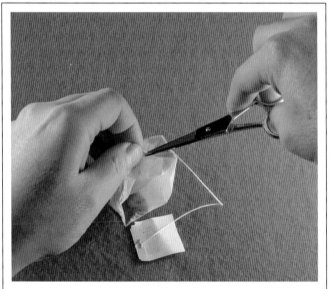

- Obtain a Lipton tea bag. Carefully remove it from the paper envelope, including the string and little tag.

- Using your left thumb and first finger, pinch away the outermost layer of the paper and make a small snip through it with the tip of a scissors about ¼ inch down from the top of the bag.

Step 2

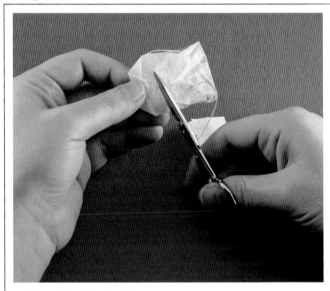

- Now, using only the tip from one blade of the scissors, cut a slit from side to side.

Ionia was literally born into a magical family. Her father was Charles de Vere, a famous Paris magic dealer and manufacturer of magic props, and her mother performed throughout Europe as Okita, with an artistic Oriental magic act. Ionia appeared as the Goddess of Mystery, dressed as an Egyptian princess, and performed tricks with parasols, fish bowls, and cages of pigeons. One of her specialties was pouring any drink requested by the audience from a glass jug of water. Reviewers commented on her cleverness and performance skills. Her career lasted only about ten years, but she certainly matched her brother magicians in ability.

Step 3

- Slide a quarter into the slit and push it down among the tea leaves.

- For those deeply motivated, you could forgo these steps by carefully opening the small staple at the top of the tea bag, inserting the quarter through the open top, and then returning the staple to the same spot and closing it.

Step 4

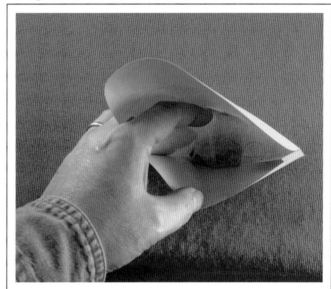

- Place the tea bag upright inside a small open envelope, then place that in a pocket or purse.

QUARTER TO TEA (continued)

Now that you're prepared, the trick still doesn't start until the situation is set. Your job is to be patient and wait until the moment is right, everyone is relaxed, and no one is expecting anything unusual. You may even be all ready to perform this trick and decide not to do it because it just doesn't seem like the right moment in the conversation ever comes up, or it would be awkward to interject into what is perhaps a serious conversation. Picking the right moment (and avoiding the wrong one) is very important when performing magic in an informal setting.

A good time to bring in the prepared tea bag is when someone tells a joke and everyone laughs (laughter is great misdirection) or when someone asks where the bathroom is (people inevitably pay attention to this information in case they need to go themselves later on).

Step 5

- Once set up, you can perform this seemingly impromptu miracle at any time. If you're in a restaurant and having tea after dinner, that's perfect. If you're at a friend's house for tea—great. Remember that until you actually put a quarter on the table, no one will have any idea that you're going to do a trick. And it's not until the end of the trick that people will realize the tea bag has anything to do with it. But you'll have to wait until the tea cup and tea bag have been placed in front of you to start.

Step 6

- So, you need to get the prepared tea bag "in play" in a casual way—and you must realize that no one will be paying any attention to you this early.
- At some point, get the tea bag out of your pocket or purse and into your lap.

68

Step 7

- When you're offered a choice of tea bags, simply take the small package in which it comes and lean back in your chair, naturally allowing your hands to fall into your lap.

- While you are conversing with your friend, tear open the small envelope as you normally would. But don't remove the tea bag inside. Instead, pick up the prepared tea bag from your lap and put it straight into your tea cup of hot water.

Step 8

Tossing aside the crumpled envelope with the unprepared tea bag inside may seem bold, but you must remember that no one has any reason to think there's anything in it because everyone has seen you remove a tea bag. It's a natural action and cuts off further thought.

- The quarter will not be visible as long as you keep the side of the bag with the slit toward you.

- Crumple up the envelope in which the other tea bag just came (with the tea bag still in it) and place it on the table off to the side. No one will pay any attention to it.

QUARTER TO TEA (continued)

Hey, the trick finally starts! This is a good example of how magicians versus the audience look at a trick. For the audience, a trick doesn't start until the magician visibly begins a sequence of events that culminates in a miracle. For the magician, the trick starts with the preparation and continues with vigilance to assess when the best moment to begin the performance arises. This is no different than a play: For the audience, the play starts when the curtain goes up. For the actors, the play starts when they audition, are chosen, receive the script, memorize their lines, rehearse, and so on.

This effect is an excellent example of learning to take your time. Don't be in a hurry to do a trick—often it's best to wait

Step 9

- And now you wait. Talk to your friend, allow your tea to steep. Have a cookie.

- After a while, ask your friend if he has a quarter you can borrow. Place it on the table in position for the vanish described just before this trick—about 3 inches from the table edge near you.

Step 10

- Perform the "vanish" exactly as explained, allowing the quarter to fall into your lap.

- Move your right hand a few inches above your tea cup and crumple your thumb and fingers magically, as if making the quarter dissolve. Show your hand empty.

until someone asks to see something magical. With this coin in a tea bag, take advantage and get all the dirty work explained on the preceding pages done while people are sitting, relaxed, and chatting. The perfect time to do things that should remain unseen is when no one is paying attention to you. Look for opportunities when attention is on someone else to get ready. Whatever you do, don't do anything while people are looking at you.

Step 11

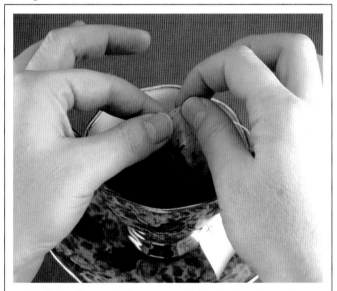

- Lift the tea bag out of your cup by its string, letting the excess tea drip off the bottom for a few seconds and allowing it to cool a bit.

- Grasp the bag just to the left of the slit between the thumbs and fingers of both hands.

Step 12

- Tear the bag open along your previously made slit. This opens the tea bag and simultaneously destroys the evidence.

- Wriggle the bag with both hands and force the quarter up into view—it should push up through the tea leaves for the best effect.

- Lean forward and hold the tea bag over a saucer. Insert the tip of a fork or knife into the bag and slowly lift out the clump of tea with the quarter in the middle.

- Brush off the tea and return the quarter to your friend.

MATRIX

Here's the professional method for one of the greatest coin tricks ever invented

(Created by Al Schneider)

The idea of having four coins arranged in a square on the table assemble under a playing card was invented by the oddly named vaudeville performer Yank Hoe at the turn of the twentieth century. He was also famous for tearing and restoring his turban. Although there have been many versions

of the trick created since then (magicians love to noodle around and make hundreds of variations of a trick), none has been as influential as Matrix, created by the brilliant close-up magician Al Schneider. Although it's among the easier versions of the trick—and everything is relative—it is one of the most difficult tricks in this book. So take your time; read and

Step 1

- Arrange the four quarters in a square formation on the table, each about 1 foot apart from the other.

- Hold the four cards face down in your right hand between the thumb, above, and fingers, beneath. Using your right thumb, spread the cards to the left so all four are visible.

Step 2

- Move both hands to the coin at the outer left corner of the square.

- Lower the card that is spread farthest to the left directly over that coin. Use your left fingertips to hold the leftmost card in place so it falls onto the coin as your right hand pulls the

lower three cards away.

- Repeat exactly the same thing, placing a card over the coin at the outer right corner of the square.

learn it slowly to make sure you've got it just right. You need four quarters, four playing cards, and a soft surface on which to perform. The surface can be a cloth napkin opened on the tabletop, a towel, or a plush tablecloth.

From now on, transparent cards are used in all the photos so you can see what's happening under them. Remember that because you will be using regular opaque playing cards, the secret will be hidden from the audience even though you can see it here.

Step 3

Step 4

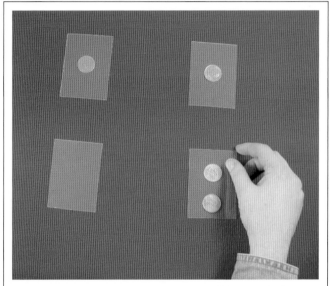

- Here comes the first sleight: Move your right hand over the coin at the inner-left corner. As before, your left fingers press down on the upper card. What changes now is that your right second and third fingertips (hidden beneath the two cards that remain) nip the coin between them. Do this by pressing down on the forward edge of the coin with your right second finger, enabling your third finger to slip under the inner edge.

- While your left hand holds the upper card in place on the table, as if it's covering the coin, your right hand moves to the right with that coin secretly beneath the remaining card. Place the right hand's card, and the hidden coin, over the coin at the inner-right corner.

- Be careful not to let the two coins accidentally **touch** and make a noise.

MATRIX (continued)

You've completed the first part of the routine: covering four coins with four cards. However, in the process, you have secretly stolen the coin from the inner-left corner and added it to the coin at the inner-right corner—unseen by the audience, of course, because the playing cards cover everything. Now comes the most difficult part of the routine, learning Schneider's Pick-Up Move, the sleight upon which the rest of the routine depends. So this page will be devoted solely to learning this important sleight, which you must be able to do with both hands.

Now you have to master the Pick-Up Move by practicing it repeatedly until you can do it without any hesitation. The audience should have absolutely no hint that there is anything under the card. Once you've mastered the Pick-Up Move, you'll be able to adapt it to many tricks.

Step 5

Remember: The cards are transparent only so you can see what's happening!

- The Pick-Up Move: Because most of you are right-handed, I'll explain it that way. Angle the outer ends of all four cards about 30 degrees toward the center. Your right hand gently grasps the outer right card at the centers of the long sides between the thumb (inner long side) and second finger (outer long side).

- Your first finger rests gently on top.

Step 6

- Slide the card diagonally outward and to the right until the edge of the quarter beneath it hits your thumb.

WHO INVENTED THIS?

Al Schneider is one of the most famous magicians in our field. Having written many books detailing his own creations, he takes great pleasure in sharing his ideas with others. His Matrix routine was first published in my magazine *Genii* in 1968. Since then it has become, in various versions, the most popular trick in the last fifty years. Al invents tricks with almost any kind of object—he has a unique gift for looking at things and seeing them in a new way.

Step 7

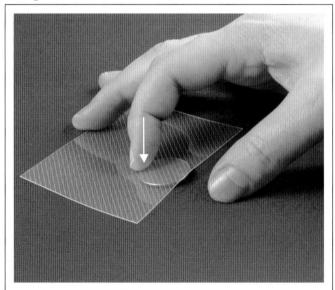

- Push downward with your first finger, pressing on the outer edge of the coin through the card and causing the inner end to rise slightly. (The thumb has been moved out of the way in the photo so you can see the coin).

Step 8

- This enables your right thumb tip to raise the inner end of the coin, and you can grasp it (and the card) between the thumb and first finger as you raise the card and allow the outer long side to snap off the second finger.

- The coin is now hidden on the side of the card facing you.

- Replace the coin and card back in their original positions, and you're ready to continue learning the trick.

MATRIX (continued)

Having mastered the essential sleight, you're ready to make all four coins magically gather under one card.

Now that you've secretly "displaced" the coin from under the inner-left corner to under the card at the inner-right corner, this puts you (as magicians say) "one ahead."

Remember that from the point of view of the audience, nothing has happened yet except that you have covered the four coins with four cards. The magical part of the trick is only now about to start.

Step 9

- Snap your right fingers over the outer-right card. Your right hand descends over it while your left hand descends over the inner-right card. Your right hand executes the Pick-Up Move while your left hand lifts its card, but only simulating the Pick-Up Move (that is, allowing the right long side to snap off your left second finger): The coin under the outer-right card has vanished, and two coins are seen under the inner-right card.

- Toss the left hand's card off to the side, face up.

Step 10

- Your right hand lowers its card, face down, over the two coins at the inner-right corner. Be careful that the third quarter does not clink against the two coins already there.

- Snap your fingers over the card at the outer left. Your left hand grasps that card while your right hand grasps the card at inner right.

- Your left hand executes the Pick-Up Move while your right hand lifts its card, simulating the Pick-Up Move: The coin under the outer-left card has vanished, and three coins are seen under the inner-right card.

Step 11

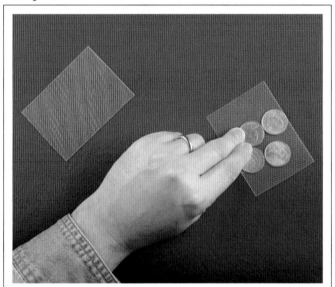

- Toss the right hand's card off to the side, face up.

- Your left hand lowers its card, face down, over the three coins at the inner-right corner. Be careful that the fourth quarter does not clink against the three coins already there.

Step 12

- Snap your left fingers over the card at the inner-left corner. Your left hand grasps the card at inner left while your right hand grasps the card at inner right.

- No need to do a sleight this time: Your left hand simulates the Pick-Up Move and lifts the inner-left card, while your right hand simulates the Pick-Up Move as it lifts the inner-right card: All four coins are now seen beneath the inner right card, completing the routine.

- Toss the two face up cards to the table to end.

ATOMIC COINS

Causing coins to penetrate a tabletop is a popular but difficult trick, so here's an easy way to do it

The plots for magic tricks can be divided into a few basic categories: Things can vanish, appear, change, transport, and penetrate. I'm simplifying things for you, but you get the point. Coins Through the Table is a classic routine that, along with Matrix, is in the repertoires of professional magicians the world over. Even though I've created the following routine so

it's simpler than most of the other methods available, much time should be taken in practicing the individual sleights and then combining them into a seamless whole.

Step 1

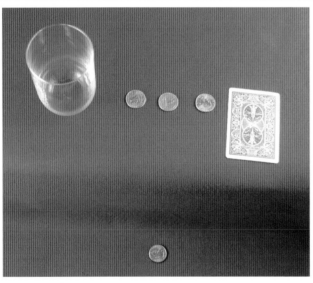

- Begin with one quarter in your lap.

- The other three quarters are on the table, along with a playing card and a glass.

Step 2

The card is transparent in this photo so you can see the position of the three coins under it.

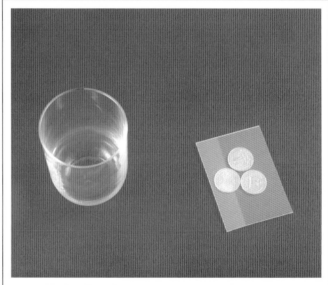

- Explain that the coins are going to travel through the table one at a time and fall into the glass.

- Arrange the quarters in a tight triangle, then cover them with the playing card so the quarter on the left is in position for the Pick-Up Move.

You need four quarters for this, but the audience will be aware of only three.

You also need a fairly small clear drinking glass. And it must be glass, not plastic, so the coins make a nice "clink" when they drop into it. The sound marks the moment of their magical passage through the table.

You'll use Al Schneider's Pick-Up Move for this unique version of Coins Through the Table, so make sure you've studied and practiced it thoroughly as explained in Matrix.

Step 3

- Your left hand picks up the glass, holding it between the thumb on one side, third and fourth fingers on the other side.

- Your first and second fingers are next to the third and fourth fingers, but they don't support the glass.

Step 4

- Move your left hand under the table and secretly pick up the coin in your lap with your left first and second fingertips.

- Your first and second fingers, now holding the coin, curl slightly so the coin is directly over the glass.

ATOMIC COINS (continued)

I've chosen to call this version of Coins Through the Table Atomic Coins because it sounds more interesting and might give you an idea for patter to accompany your actions. You can talk about how you're causing the coins to break down into their original atomic substructure in order to move between the atoms of the table (or some other exotic nonsense). Say this tongue-in-cheek, of course, because it's silly. You don't want an intelligent spectator to feel insulted that you're trying to pass off such obviously bogus science as fact.

Step 5

- Snap your right fingers over the playing card, and, an instant later, your left first and second fingers allow the coin to fall into the glass with a clink.

- Your right hand executes the Pick-Up Move, lifting the card with one of the three quarters secretly hidden behind it.

Step 6

- Your left hand brings the glass above the table and spills out the coin somewhat off to the left. At the same time, your right hand moves back just past the table edge and allows the coin hidden behind it to drop into your lap. During this move, make sure you dip the lower long side

of the playing card below the edge of the table so the coin isn't seen by the audience when it falls from behind the card.

KNACK MAGIC TRICKS

80

Remember that both hands move in concert— your left hand leads to draw the eyes of the audience, and your right hand begins its journey only a second later. Do not perform the activities as if they are separate steps, one after another.

Step 7

- Your left hand takes the glass under the table, secretly picking up the coin from your lap with the first and second fingertips as before.

- Your right hand covers the two coins with the card.

- Now repeat the same sequence: Snap your right fingers, your left fingers allow the coin to fall into the glass, and do the Pick-Up Move to show only one coin under the card.

Step 8

- Your left hand comes up with the glass and spills the second coin onto the table so it falls onto the first coin off to the left. At the same time, your right hand moves inward past the table edge and allows the coin hidden behind the card to drop into your lap.

- Again, make sure that the lower long side of the card is below the edge of the table so the coin isn't seen as it falls.

ATOMIC COINS (continued)

It's time to change gears and alter the method before the audience gets wise. That's the difference between an "effect" and a "routine." Whereas an effect consists of a single magical event, a routine consists of several magical events—sometimes it's the same event repeated two or three times, as is the case here. In order to stay a step ahead of the spectators, you change methods.

Another lesson: Don't use the same method too many times in a row. In this case, using the Pick-Up Move to vanish a coin from under a card twice is the limit. More than that, and the audience may figure out what you're doing. You see, spectators are like students: They learn from watching you. So it's a good idea to use a different method to cause the third coin to penetrate the table. That's easy enough by substituting a different sleight.

Step 9

- Your left hand takes the glass and goes under the table a final time—pick up the coin from your lap with your left first and second fingertips, holding it over the mouth of the glass.

- Say, *"This time we won't use the card,"* as your right hand places it aside.

- Position the remaining coin about 5 inches from the table edge in position for a clever way to vanish a coin invented by Canadian magician Ross Bertram: Rubdown.

Step 10

The position of the coin under your hand is shown with a dotted line.

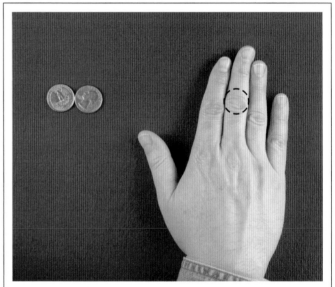

- Place your right hand palm down, fingers together and straight, flatly over the coin—it should be under your fingers.

Step 11

You can see the coin through the hand in this photo—a bit of magic in itself.

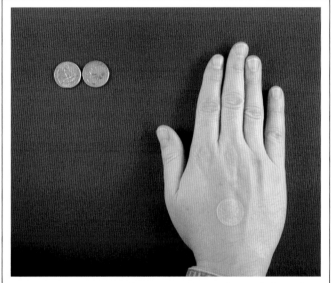

- Begin moving your right hand in small, counterclockwise, circular motions—you'll find that the coin will work itself back under your hand. The hand itself does not move inward other than in its circular motion.

- Keep going, and after a few moments the coin will have moved all the way back to your wrist.

Step 12

Ross Bertram's Rubdown Move, which is how your right hand maneuvers the coin back to the table edge, requires only small circular movements. Four circular motions should do it. If you have to make eight, then enlarge the motion, requiring fewer movements.

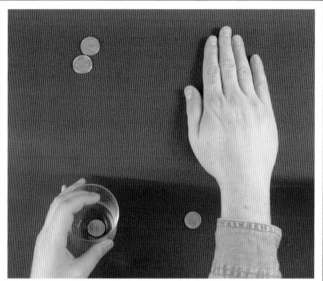

- Make a final rubbing motion to send the coin over the edge of the table and into your lap. Your left first and second fingers allow their coin to drop into the glass with a clink.

- Once that sound is heard, lift your right hand to reveal that the coin that was beneath it is now gone. Bring the glass above the table and spill out the third coin.

THERE'S MONEY IN BAKED GOODS

You can find more than raisins and nuts in a good dinner roll

In this fun effect, you borrow a quarter and write your initials on it. The quarter vanishes completely. You pick up a roll from the bread basket, break it open, and the initialed quarter is discovered inside.

Before you can perform this trick, you need to have mastered A Coin Vanish in chapter 6. You also need a quarter, a permanent marker, and a dinner roll or muffin. This is best performed someplace like a restaurant or dinner table where rolls will already be present.

Step 1

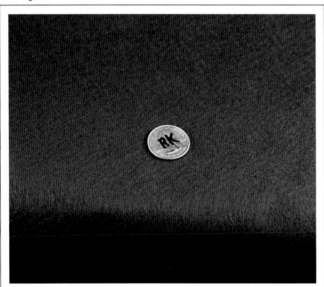

- In advance, write your initials on the heads side of the quarter. Do it in a way so you can exactly duplicate the initials later. This quarter and the marker should be in your left jacket pocket.

- At some point later in the meal, ask if you can borrow

a quarter from someone. Place it on the table, heads side up, about 3 inches from the edge nearest you. Remove the marker from your left pocket and write your initials on the quarter—try to do it in exactly the same way that you wrote them on the first quarter.

Step 2

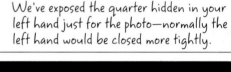

We've exposed the quarter hidden in your left hand just for the photo—normally the left hand would be closed more tightly.

- Recap the marker and put it back into your left jacket pocket. Once you've let go of the marker, pick up the quarter.

- Let it rest inside your naturally curled fingers. After your left hand emerges from the pocket, it moves straight to the table and rests there casually.

It's possible, but more difficult, to do this trick and allow the spectator to sign the quarter. First, borrow the quarter and have it signed by someone. Second, vanish the quarter (same method) so it ends up in your lap. Third, show both hands empty and let them drop in your lap as you lean forward with interest while the spectator selects a roll from the breadbasket. Fourth, while in your lap your left hand secretly retrieves the coin (same position in the hand) and ascends to the table. Fifth, accept the roll from the spectator with your right hand and finish as explained.

Don't forget to make sure your initials are seen by the audience either when the coin comes out of the roll or right afterward. But don't make a big deal out of it.

Step 3

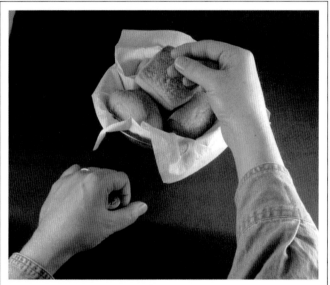

- Lower your right fingers, held together and straight, over the initialed quarter on the table and vanish it, dragging it off the table so it falls into your lap. Your right thumb and fingers, held as if the coin is still inside them, are moved above the breadbasket. With a magical gesture, rub your thumb and fingers together and reveal that the quarter has vanished. Ask someone to pick up any roll or muffin from the basket and hand it to you.

Step 4

- Take the roll with your right hand. Because your intention is to break the roll, it's natural for you to lean back and grasp the left side of the roll with your left hand, thumb above and fingers beneath. The concealed quarter rests on your left fingers under the roll. Press both thumbs down into the center of the roll while simultaneously pushing upward with the fingers of both hands. This breaks the roll and reveals the quarter. Push it upward through the roll with your fingers into view.

ANYTIME TRICKS

MEET URI GELLER

Bending spoons isn't just for mentalists

You borrow a spoon from someone sitting at your table and, with great effort, bend it completely in half. Realizing that this is bad behavior in a restaurant, you restore the spoon to its original condition.

This is an old effect whose origin is unknown; however, it was greatly improved by Dai Vernon's son Derek, who added a little something (five cents' worth) that makes it much more convincing.

Step 1

- Sitting at a table, have a nickel hidden in your lap before you start.

- Explain, *"You may have heard of or seen that famous guy Uri Geller who bends spoons using mind power. I don't mess with mind power, though."*

Step 2

Again, we've left the nickel visible inside the left fingers just for the photo—your fingers should be closed more tightly so it isn't seen.

- Ask someone if you can borrow a spoon. Let your left hand drop into your lap as you extend your right hand to take the spoon. The nickel should rest inside the curled fingers of your left hand.

- Once your right hand has the spoon, raise your left hand to the table as you lean back in your seat.

The plot of bending a spoon as a so-called psychic effect was created by Israeli performer Uri Geller and popularized by him in the 1970s. He claims to bend a spoon by using some ambiguous "power," and you think you see it bending by itself. In my opinion he is one of the greatest close-up magicians of the past fifty years, but he will never call himself a "magician." His method for bending a spoon is not what's described here, but this older method (where you openly bend a spoon and restore it) dovetails nicely with some Uri Geller patter for entertainment.

Step 3

- Lower the spoon so the tip is touching the table and the concave area of the bowl is facing the audience.

- Say, *"Who needs mind power when you can just use brute force?"*

Step 4

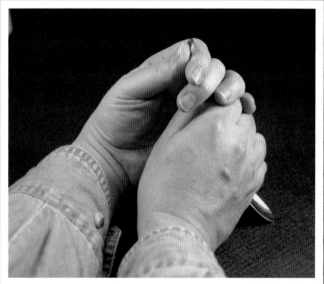

- Your right hand makes a fist around the handle just above the bowl. Wrap your left fingers around the upper end of the handle, at the same time pushing the nickel upward with your thumb so just a tiny bit of its rim is in view above the edge of your left first finger—it appears to be the end of the spoon's handle.

- The actual end of the spoon is concealed inside your curled left fingers.

MEET URI GELLER (continued)

Okay, you're set up and in position. Now it's time for some good acting so you don't look silly. You know what it's like to see someone attempting to convince you of one thing when something else is obviously true: It's called "lying." Well, your body can lie just as well as your mouth, and if you don't appear to make a genuine effort to bend the spoon, the audience will perceive your action as a lie, and someone will simply say, "You're not bending the spoon!" That's the kiss of death to a successful performance. So, buy some cheap spoons and practice by actually bending them so you learn what it feels like to do really do it. Then you have a frame of reference for the fake action.

Step 5

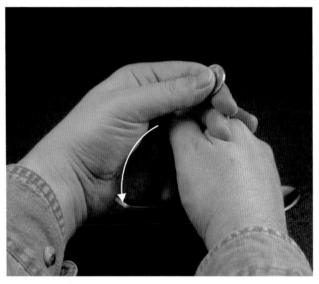

- Lean into the spoon as if you are going to bend it. Press firmly downward with both hands.

- Let the spoon's handle slip past your left fingers and move downward so that the whole spoon lies flatly on the table under your right hand.

Step 6

Here's what it looks like to the audience.

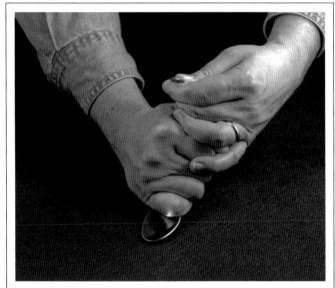

- Because the nickel is masquerading as the top of the spoon's handle, it looks like you've bent the bowl at a right angle.

- Say, *"Uri Geller spent years learning how to bend a spoon with his mind. My method is much simpler!"*

•••• VARIATION ••••

If you don't have a nickel handy, you can still perform this trick and get almost as good an illusion. Simply ignore all the instructions involving the nickel and bend and restore the spoon as described on this page.

Step 7

- As you turn both hands palm down over the spoon, your left thumb slides the nickel inside the hand so it's no longer visible as you say, *"But Uri Geller never does this...."*

Step 8

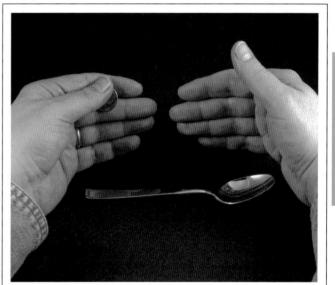

- After you pull your hands back so that people can see the straightened spoon on the table, casually put your hands into your pockets. While they are there, drop the nickel. You can also, if you're seated at the table, allow the nickel to drop into your lap. Acting as if the spoon has become superheated in its restoration gives you a reason to suddenly drop it and pull your hands away.

ANYTIME TRICKS

JUMPING RUBBER BAND

Here's one of the simplest yet most visible "anytime" magic tricks ever invented

(Created by Stanley Collins)

Here is a neat trick: Short and sweet—a rubber band that encircles your first and second fingers jumps, in the blink of an eye, to your third and fourth fingers.

Although you can hold your right hand perfectly still when you straighten and close your fingers, you can also make that action less visible by covering it (a small action) with a larger action. For example, quickly pass your left hand in front of your right hand at the exact moment when you straighten and close your right fingers, or swing your right hand from side to side while you straighten and close your fingers.

Step 1

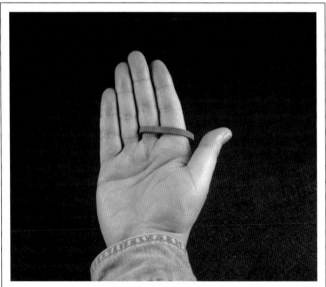

- You need a rubber band, preferably not tan (a dark color makes it easier to see), that is about 1½ inches in diameter. But it really depends on the size of your hand. The rubber band should not be too loose as you follow the instructions.

- (If you're teaching this to a child, make sure you use a small rubber band, or else it will lead to frustration.)

- Begin by looping the band over your right first and second fingers.

Step 2

- Using your left thumb and fingers, pull the band toward you and curl all of your right fingers, inserting them into the loop.

Stanley Collins was a performer, creator, and author of magic books at the beginning of the twentieth century. He was a notorious curmudgeon—a cranky old man—but damned clever. When he invented this simple trick, little did he know it would be the thing that outlived him (often unncredited) in almost every magic book written for the public nearly a century later.

Step 3

- Release the end of the band held by your left thumb and fingers.

Step 4

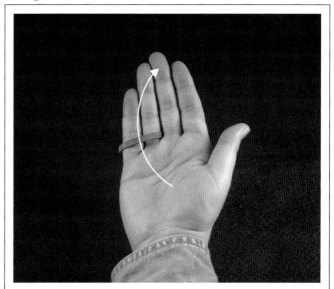

- Open your right fingers very rapidly, and the band will jump onto your third and fourth fingers.

- Immediately close the fingers again. Your fingers should snap open and shut in a flash.

ANYTIME TRICKS

VOODOO BURN
Ponder the impossibility of creating the illusion that you've just burned yourself without a flame

(Created by Jack Kent Tillar)

The spectator lights a match, blows it out, and then presses it onto a drawing of your thumb. A second later a large blister appears on your real thumb. This may be a simple trick to do, like Meet Uri Geller, where you bend and restore a spoon, but it also requires acting ability to make it believable. If you don't react (not overreact, but react *believably*) when the spectator apparently causes a blister to appear on your finger, the trick simply has no meaning, because you will have failed to convince the audience that the blister is real. Blisters hurt! Remember that.

Step 1

- You need a key with a round hole in the top.

- This is in your right jacket or trousers pocket. (If you're standing, use your trousers pocket; if you're sitting, use your jacket pocket.)

- You also need a piece of paper, a pen, and a book of matches. These are in view on the table.

Step 2

- Place your left hand, palm down, flatly on the paper.

- Trace the outline of your hand using the pen. Say to a woman who is watching, *"I'm going to turn my back for a moment. When I'm not looking, remove one of the matches from the book, light it, blow it out, and immediately press it on the thumb on the drawing. Tell me when the match is touching the thumb."*

Jack Kent Tillar was bitten by the magic bug early, doing shows when he was still in his early teens. After a stint in the armed forces, he went to work at CBS, eventually overseeing and composing the scores for many TV shows and films. All the while he continued to develop new magic, and one day he discovered a new principle—how to create the illusion of an instant blister on a fingertip. It has made him famous among magicians the world over.

Step 3

Your right hand is actually in your pocket when it does this!

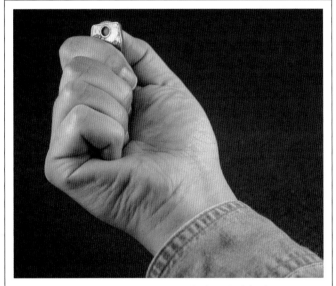

Step 4

The appearance of the faux blister is so authentic, don't be surprised if people think you're really injured.

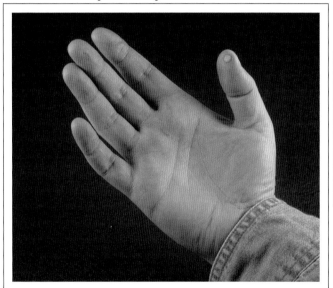

ANYTIME TRICKS

- Turn away and stick your right hand quickly into the pocket containing the key. You have strong misdirection for this: Everyone will be watching the woman follow your instructions.

- Press the tip of your right thumb very firmly against the head of the key. A portion of the flesh will fill the hole in the key—this will cause a blister-like bump to appear on your thumb after a few seconds.

- Just as the woman starts to speak, interrupt her and yell, *"Ouch!"* quite loudly.

- As you withdraw your hand from your pocket, bend over slightly to disguise the action—it appears as if you're reacting to pain.

- Face forward and extend your palm-up right hand to the woman to reveal the "blister" on your thumb.

- Ask her to extend her hand, palm up. Press your thumb firmly against her palm and rub it for ten to twelve seconds.

- When you raise your thumb, the blister will have miraculously vanished. Congratulate the woman on her amazing healing ability.

LET'S FLOAT

It's easy to leave Earth behind with this simple method of levitation

(Created by Edmund Balducci)
This method for doing an impromptu levitation had been "underground" in the magic community for many years until David Blaine performed it on his first TV special in 1997. Now you can learn it, too. It takes some practice, so don't be deceived by the brief description. You'll need good balance

and excellent presentation if you're going to make people believe you are really floating.

While all magic is a performance of the impossible, some things are just plain ridiculous—claiming you can float is one of them. Don't make this levitation the feature of your performance. We don't all have the presentational abilities of David Blaine.

Step 1

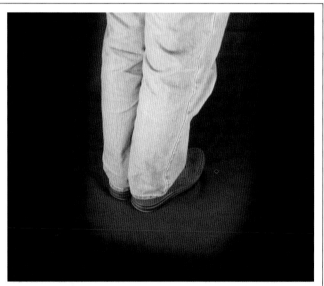

- Before performing this, you must make sure that the circumstances are suitable, because this illusion can be viewed only from a certain angle. The audience—which can consist of just one or two people—must be standing directly behind you: Anyone on the sides will see how it's done. The best situation is when you can stand in the corner of a room, facing the intersection where the walls meet.

- Take about ten good-size steps away from the spectator and angle yourself to the left about 45 degrees—in other words, turn to 10 o'clock.

Step 2

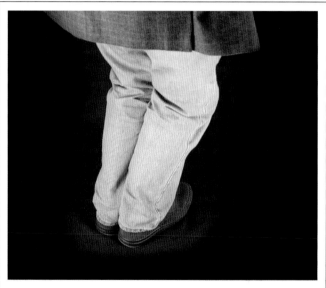

- Hold your arms straight out from your sides and breathe deeply in and out through your mouth (loudly enough so that it can be heard). Crouch slightly.

- Your acting must be convincing, or else you'll look foolish.

WHO INVENTED THIS?

Edmund Balducci was a close friend of Dai Vernon and one of the inner circle of magicians in New York City for most of the twentieth century. A civil engineer by day, he created and performed magic for friends for many years. Although he was the first to publish this method for self-levitation, he never claimed its invention. Even so, it bears his name.

It's not how long you remain elevated that's important but rather how well you've convinced the spectator that you've really floated up in the air—even if only for a few seconds.

Step 3

- Simultaneously lower your arms to your sides, exhale loudly, and press downward with the toes of your left foot, elevating your right heel.

- Your entire right foot (toes included) rises along with your left heel. Because you have turned to the left, the spectator sees your entire right foot off the ground. Because the left heel is also off the ground, it appears as if you're floating.

Step 4

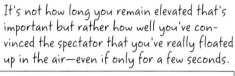

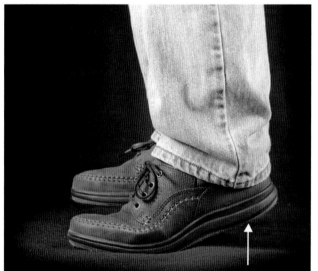

- This photo shows an exposed side view of how your left toes remain on the ground while everything else rises.

- Because you're balancing on the toes of one foot, you'll be able to stay up for only a few seconds. Slowly let yourself down, at the same time raising your arms and loudly Inhaling, crouching a bit as you land: This makes it appear as if you floated higher than you actually did.

FANTASTIC STRING TRICK

Tricks that in some way involve the spectator at the moment of magic always make a big impression

(Created by Harry Kellar and Karl Germain)
This is a seemingly simple trick: Two separate strings are shown and become one. It has a devious method: There is never more than one piece of string. The way it works is clever because it relies on the inherent characteristic of a certain type of cotton string. It does need to be prepared in advance; however, the gimmick literally disappears into the string during the climactic moment of the effect. It has its roots in a trick performed by the conjuror Karl Germain in the early part of the nineteenth century, but this exact method, simplified from the original, was developed by an unknown magician sometime after that. Its only weak point is that the

Step 1

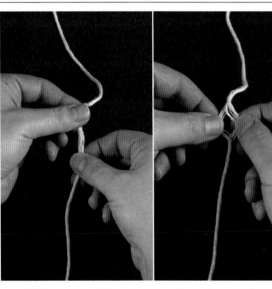

- Hold the center of the string between your fingers and untwist it a little— you'll see the strands start to separate.

- Grasp the strands and pull them apart.

Step 2

- Twist the pulled-out pieces between the thumbs and fingers. Two short pieces will now stick out at right angles from the main string.

- You have just created two false "ends." Angle the false ends upward and the real ends downward, and it appears as if you have two pieces of string, each about 9 inches long.

strings are never held any real distance apart in the early part of the trick, and I've attempted to solve that by adding an amusing presentation that enables you to switch real separate strings for your prepared string in a simple way.

At your local hardware store, obtain cotton string made up of multiple strands—if you look closely at the string you'll be able to clearly see the strands circling around it. You need a piece 18 inches long.

We've left the strings sticking out in the photo so you can see where they go, but make sure to push them all the way inside before you start.

Step 3

- You need two number 10 business-size white envelopes. One you keep as is. From the other, cut away everything but the large solid front panel (the side on which you would normally write the address).

- Now trim a tiny bit off all four sides and slip the large piece inside the whole envelope. You have created a "flap envelope" that can be used for switching things—in this case, pieces of string.

Step 4

- Place your prepared string in the envelope on one side of the flap.

- On the other side of the flap, place two unprepared pieces of string, each 9 inches long. Now you are ready to begin.

FANTASTIC STRING TRICK (continued)

Advance preparation completed, you're ready to do magic.

Although the gag with the envelope may seem unimportant, it serves an important purpose. Not only does it allow you to make a joke, but it also shows two genuinely separate strings. That's vital to the success of the trick when, at the end, the strings become one.

Step 5

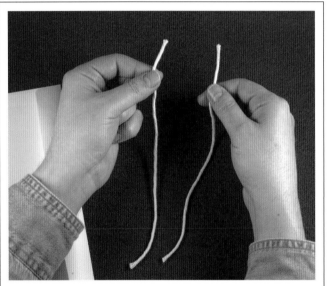

- A few minutes before you perform this, bring out the envelope, open it with the interior toward you, and take out the two 9-inch strings. Say, *"Let me show you this fantastic string trick . . . no, it's too good. I can't show it to you yet."* Both strings are seen as separate. Stuff them into the envelope (same side of the flap as before) and put it away.

Step 6

Just like before, the separate strings go on the far side of the flap.

- Now do another trick. Afterward, take out the envelope and repeat exactly the same business, taking out the two single strings, saying the same thing, then putting them back into the envelope and putting it away.

- Do another trick. Afterward, bring out the envelope a third time and say, *"You've been a really good audience, so I guess it's time I showed you the Fantastic String Trick."*

Harry Kellar was America's favorite magician by the end of the 1800s. Born in Erie, Pennsylvania, Kellar was known for having a friendly, genial manner onstage and for bringing his audiences astonishing mysteries, many of which he purchased, or purloined, from the great European magicians of the day. This poster advertises a tiny wooden cabinet that was supposedly inhabited by ghosts, "spiritualism" being the great fad of the day. A bell and tambourine placed inside the empty cabinet played by themselves; writing appeared on a slate; and a borrowed pocket handkerchief danced out of the cabinet as if haunted.

Step 7

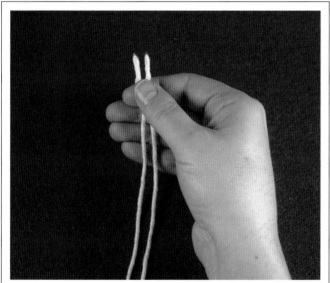

- Open the envelope and this time bring out the prepared string. Your right hand holds it at the juncture where the fake ends meet, your right thumb covering the join. The prepared string looks identical to the separate strings.

- Your left hand puts the envelope back into your pocket.

- Ask a spectator to grasp the lower ends of the string, one in each hand. Say, *"Please raise your hands and slowly move them apart."*

Step 8

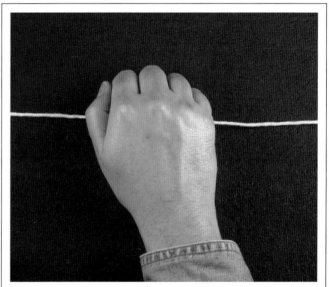

- With your right thumb, draw the small ends of the string inside your hand, then turn your closed fist palm down. One end of the string should emerge from each side.

- Ask the spectator to slowly pull the ends—he's actually pulling the string back to normal position so the small ends reincorporate themselves into the string where they began.

- Rub the string inside your fist during this to help the strands return to their original position. Then, open your hand and reveal that the string is now one piece.

STRING TRICKS

RING, STRING, ZING!

This impossible penetration of a spectator's finger ring onto a string is startling

(Created by Stewart James)

Place a string on the table and cover the center with a hanky. Borrow a finger ring and place it and a small safety pin under the handkerchief. The ends of the string remain in full view at all times. When the string is pulled out from under the hanky, the finger ring is magically linked onto it.

Although we have used a sheer piece of cloth in the photographs so you can see what happens underneath, when you perform this trick you must use an opaque handkerchief.

Step 1

- You need a piece of string, an opaque handkerchief, and a small safety pin.

Step 2

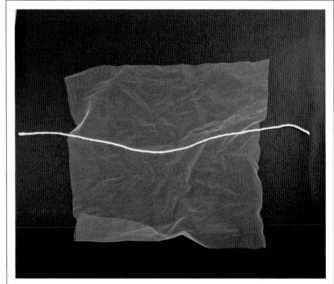

- Lay the string horizontally across the table so the ends are to the right and left.

- Open the handkerchief and place it over the center of the string. It's important that both ends of the string stick out from under the sides of the handkerchief.

Step 3

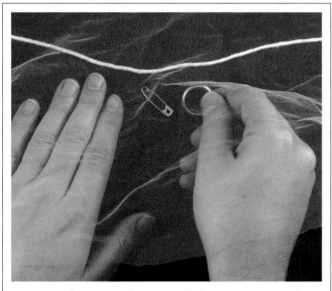

- Borrow a finger ring of any type from a spectator.

- Bring out the safety pin and drop it onto the table.

- Pick up the ring and safety pin, then slip your hands under the hanky. Put down the safety pin so you hold only the ring.

Step 4

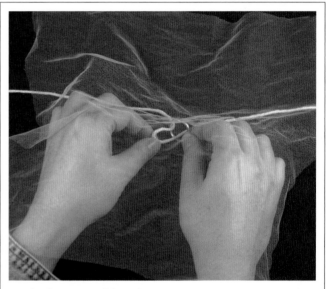

- Take the center of the string and pull it through the ring, creating a loop.

RING, STRING, ZING! (continued)

This effect is unusual because the spectators don't know what you're going to do until after it's done.

Although the physical part of doing magic is not much different than, say, learning to slice an apple without cutting yourself, the psychological part adds an entirely separate dimension. There is no magic without mystery. They are inseparable. Mystery is the very thing that's missing from a puzzle, which is why it's so important in your presentation to add mystery to your tricks. One of the ways you can do that is by having part of the action take place out of sight, such as in an envelope or in your pocket or in this case under a handkerchief. If properly played, the spectators will be curious almost to the point of bother by what you're doing under the hanky, but they should never be annoyed by it. That's where your personality comes in.

Step 5

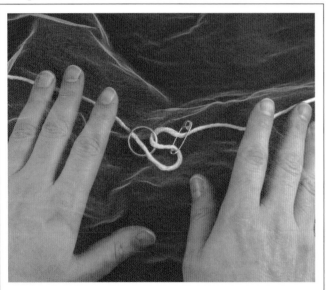

- Pick up the safety pin and open it. Stick the staff of the pin through the two strings (the point must pierce the center of each strand) to the right of the loop you've just made.

- Because you can't see under the handkerchief, it will take practice to do this without sticking yourself. Be careful!

Step 6

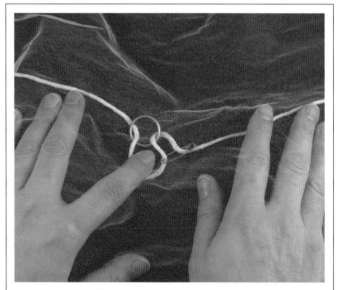

- Stick your left first finger into the loop of string you created a moment ago and press it firmly against the table.

Fredrick Bancroft was an amateur magician and a wealthy Minnesota dentist who decided to become a professional entertainer. He styled his show after that of Alexander Herrmann and spent lavishly on equipment and advertising posters. He even included an illusion with a live lion. This poster is an example of Bancroft's lavish taste. Actually, his stage setting was never this elaborate (the poster artist exaggerated the show's scenery), but Bancroft portrayed himself as a masterful wizard. He never got the chance to prove it. Just several years after his premiere, he died of typhoid fever in 1897.

Step 7

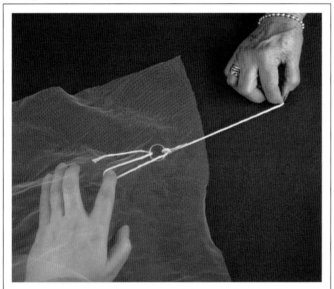

- Ask a spectator to slowly pull the right end of the string. Once it's taut, the safety pin will press on the ring and hold it in place against the string as it emerges from beneath the handkerchief.

- Keep your left first finger in the loop until the string has snaked all the way around it.

Step 8

- When you feel the end of the string with your left fingers, quickly grab it, then pull the handkerchief away with your right hand so the audience can see that the ring has magically become linked to the string.

- Remove the safety pin. It isn't until you do this that the ring is clearly seen to be on the string.

- Wait a few moments for the effect to sink in, then slide the ring off the string and return it to the proper spectator.

STRAW 'N' STRING

This is a close-up version of the classic Cut and Restored Rope

(Created by Joseph Kolar)

Here's a conundrum: You have no rope and no heavy-duty scissors, but you want to cut and restore a rope. This close-up version of the famous trick is made extremely easy by the

addition of a drinking straw—an ingenious solution developed by Joseph Kolar in the 1920s.

A piece of string is slid into the straw. The straw is folded in half and cut at the center. The two pieces of the cut straw are

Remember: The line I've drawn on the straw to mark the slit is only so you can see where it is in the photos. Don't draw a line on your straw.

Step 1

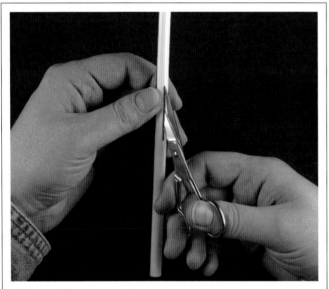

- You need an opaque plastic drinking straw, a piece of string, and a pair of scissors.

- Prepare in advance by cutting a small lengthwise slit about 1½ inches long in the middle of the straw. (I've also drawn the location of the slit on the straw with a marker so you can see it.)

Step 2

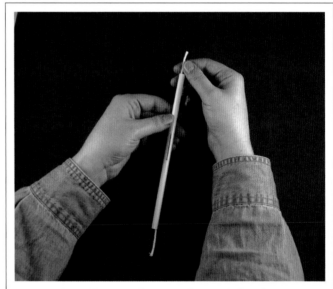

- Begin the performance by holding the straw vertically with your left hand so the slit is toward you.

- Your right hand picks up the string by one end and lowers it through the straw until it emerges from the lower end.

seen to be clearly separated, yet when you put them together and slide out the string, it is seen to be uncut. Although this is a standard trick to teach beginning magicians, it's a very good one, and I've made it even better by adapting a clever subtlety used in rope magic that enables you to hold the cut pieces of straw, with the string inside, unquestionably separated after you've cut them.

Step 3 The audience won't notice you rotating the straw.

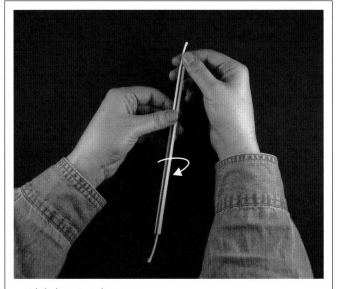

- While keeping the straw vertical, slowly rotate it between your left thumb and first finger until the hidden slit is on its right side.

Step 4 Bend the straw slowly so the spectators don't think you're doing anything suspicious.

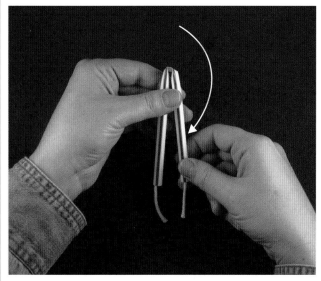

- Bend the straw in half by folding the upper part clockwise to the right.

- Hold the bent straw near the bend between your left thumb and fingers.

STRAW 'N' STRING (continued)

Even with just a string, don't neglect the psychological element of danger when you cut something. Scissors are dangerous, and even when used for comic effect, simply pointing the tips at someone close to you can cause great discomfort for that person. If you want to allow a spectator to cut the straw and string, you can, provided that you're careful. You can even get some comic byplay out of it by moving it out of his way each time he tries to cut it as if you had just one more thing that you must say before the string is cut.

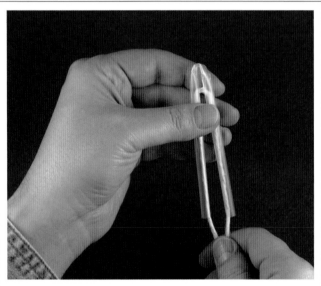

Step 5

We've used a transparent straw in this photo and the next so you can see where the string really is.

- Your right thumb and fingers grasp the lower, loose ends of the string and pull firmly downward/inward— this forces the center of the string down into the slit, where it is concealed by your left thumb and fingers.

- The audience thinks that the string is still through the center of the straw.

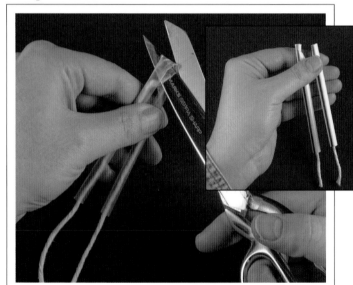

Step 6

The image shown in the inset photo is the big convincer.

- Pick up the scissors with your right hand and cut the straw in half right at the bend. Do this as openly as possible so there can be no question that you are genuinely cutting the straw. The scissors, as you can see in the photo with the transparent straw, are actually **above the string.**

- Put the scissors down. Straighten the cut halves— see inset photo. While the cut ends of the straw are visible, the uncut string is hidden under your left thumb.

The moment when you straighten the straw is when the magic occurs—snap your fingers afterward to reinforce that.

Step 7

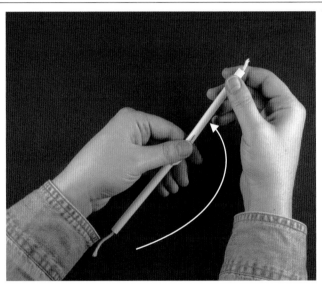

- Grasp the right half of the straw and pivot it counterclockwise until the halves form one straight piece again.

- Make sure to keep the point at which the straw was cut behind your left fingers so the string remains concealed.

Step 8

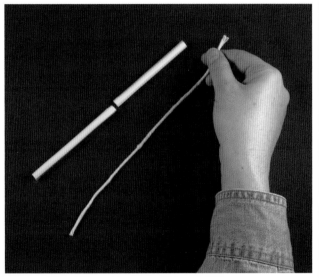

- Grasp the right end of the string with your right hand and pull it straight out of the straw in one slow motion. The "slow" pull creates tension and drama.

- The string has been miraculously restored.

IMPROMPTU MIND READING
This mystery can be done just about anyplace with ordinary objects

(Created by Roy Baker)

Seven different objects are arranged on the table: a pen, a coin, a cell phone, a spoon, a fork, a cup, and a key ring with some keys on it. The magician writes a prediction on a piece of paper, folds it in half, and places it on the table under a spectator's hand. The magician and another spectator take turns selecting objects from among the seven on the table and eliminating them. Only one object remains on the table at the end, left there by chance. Yet, when the prediction is unfolded and read aloud, you have correctly predicted which object would remain.

We had to keep the objects fairly close together for our photos, but you should definitely spread them out a bit more so your hands aren't cramped when you cover them.

Step 1

- Any odd number of different objects, with a minimum of five, can be used. Let's assume that there are seven objects: a pen, a coin, a cell phone, a spoon, a fork, a cup, and a key ring with some keys on it. These should be borrowed from spectators or taken from things already on the table. Because I'm using a fork, a spoon, and a cup, you can tell that I'm probably doing this for someone in a restaurant.

- You also need a slip of paper and a pen or marker.

Step 2

THE Keys Will Remain!

- Say, *"I am going to try a bit of mind reading with one of you in a moment. We're going to take turns and eliminate all but one of these seven objects. I'm going to predict in advance which object will remain."*

- Decide which one of the objects you want to predict—let's use the key ring as an example. Write "The Keys Will Remain" on the piece of paper without letting anyone see what you've written, fold it in half, and slide it under the hand of someone in the audience.

"Roy Baker" was the stage name of British magician Geoffrey R. H. Hursell. He was also a hypnotist and mentalist (someone who specializes in doing mental magic). He wrote half a dozen books in our field and in 1968 first published the PATEO Force principle. PATEO is an acronym for Pick Any Two, Eliminate One. Even if he never invented anything else of value (which he did), he will be long remembered for this new principle.

If you're performing for a single person, then just have that spectator put the prediction in his or her pocket so the person's hands are free.

Step 3

- Choose another spectator to assist you.

- You must go first: Cover any two objects on the table, one under your left hand, the other under your right. You may choose any two of the objects, but never choose the object you've predicted—in this case, the keys.

Step 4

- Inform the spectator that he can now tell you to discard one of the two objects beneath your hands.

- Whichever one he picks (the fork in this example), push it way off to the side.

IMPROMPTU MIND READING (continued)

Don't do this with more than nine objects, because the method might become obvious through repetition. Note that if you like to do card tricks, then you can have from seven to nine cards selected from the deck and use those. If the cards are placed on the table face up, you can simply choose one and then make a secret prediction.

Step 5

- Now, tell the spectator that it is his turn to cover two objects. He may cover the keys with one hand. If that happens, then you tell him to discard the item under his other hand. It would be the cup in the example shown in the photo.

Step 6　　　*Remember: Never, ever cover the keys!*

- The way this trick works is both simple and ingenious: You will never cover the keys, and so he can never tell you to discard them, and if he covers the keys, you tell him to discard the object under his other hand. This way, the keys never get discarded, and after you continue to do this, taking turns with the spectator, the keys will be the last item on the table.

Although extremely simple to do, the PATEO Force—Pick Any Two, Eliminate One—can also be too obvious if you don't throw a little presentation and acting into the process. Do not rush through it—it must appear to the spectator as if you're giving serious thought not only to which objects you cover but also to which objects you make him discard. Remember: You never cover the object you want to force, and if the spectator covers it, always tell him to eliminate the other object.

Step 7

The photo shows you covering the cell phone and pen.

- For example, say that you cover the coin and the fork. The spectator tells you to eliminate the fork. There are now six objects on the table.

- He covers the keys and the cup. You tell him to eliminate the cup. There are now five objects on the table.

- You cover the cell phone and the pen. He tells you to eliminate the pen. There are now four objects on the table.

Step 8

- He covers the cell phone and the coin. You tell him to eliminate the coin. There are now three objects on the table.

- You cover the cell phone and the spoon. He tells you to eliminate the cell phone.

- There are now two objects on the table. He covers the spoon and the keys.

- You tell him to eliminate the spoon. There is now one object remaining: the keys.

- When only the keys are left, ask the person to read the prediction: "The Keys Will Remain."

111

51 FACES NORTH
A prediction reveals the spectator's choice before he makes it

(Created by P. Howard Lyons)

The spectator shuffles the deck. Afterward, you take it and explain that you need a piece of paper on which to make a note. Because you don't have one, you spread through the deck and scribble something on one of the cards.

The card is placed face up on the table, and the prediction is read to the spectator—it is an "open" prediction, informing him of what card he is destined to select in the future. The

spectator begins dealing down through the deck, turning the cards face up and making a pile.

When he comes to the mate of the card on which the prediction is written, he counts down that many more cards and leaves the card at that number face down. He then deals through the balance of the deck, turning the cards face up. The predicted card is never seen. When the face-down card in the deck is examined, it is revealed to be the predicted card.

Step 1

- There is no advance preparation aside from having a marker handy. Make sure there are no bits of paper around, or else you won't have a reason to write on a playing card later in the trick.

- Ask the spectator to shuffle the deck and return it to you. Take it in dealing position in the left hand and tilt it so the faces are toward you.

Step 2

- Begin spreading through the cards, looking for a three- or four-valued spot card near the face of the deck.

- Here you can see the three of clubs is sixth from the face—we'll use that in this instance.

While you're looking for the three of spades in this particular case, you might also be looking for a different card—the mate of a red three that you originally saw near the face of the deck, or even a red or black four. Just remember that the card you look for here might be different each time you do the trick.

Step 3

Step 4

- When you find the three, count back three cards toward the face of the deck and note the card at that number—this will be your predicted card (let's assume it's the king of hearts).

- So, the king of hearts is three cards in front of the three of clubs. (Note that if you found a four within the first few cards of the deck rather than a three, you would count back four cards.)

- Continue spreading through the deck until you come to the mate of the three or four spot, and in this case you would stop when you reach the three of spades.

113

51 FACES NORTH (continued)

The plot is a bit of a mind twister: How can the future occur before the past?

Like so many simple tricks, this one demands more from you in terms of presentation and personality. There is a point where the spectator will deal through a good part of the deck in this effect; you must create dramatic tension during this by verbally pointing out that the predicted card could turn up at any moment. Every card that's turned over is an opportunity for a little bit of drama.

Step 5

- Remove this card and write "king of hearts" on it. Place it face up on the table as your "open" prediction.

Step 6

- Turn the deck face down and place it on the table. Ask the spectator to give the deck a complete cut. Then say, *"Please pick up the deck and hold it face down. Begin dealing cards to the table, turning each one face up and making a pile."*

- Tell the spectator to watch for the mate of the card on which you've written the open prediction, the three of clubs. Because he will have cut the deck at about center, he will come to the three of clubs in a relatively short period of time.

The spectator deals the third card after the three of clubs face down onto the cards on the table.

Step 7

- Say, *"The three of clubs tells you to count down three more cards, but leave the third card face down, do not turn it face up. Place it on top of the cards on the table and continue to deal through the rest of the deck turning the cards face up."* The spectator deals two more face-up cards, then a face-down card, then continues dealing through the rest of the deck, turning all the cards face up.

- He never finds the predicted king of hearts.

Step 8

- Spread the face-up deck on the table and ask the spectator to remove the one face-down card and turn it over to reveal the king of hearts—the predicted card.

THOUGHT SPELLER
This method utilizes an ancient mathematical placement in conjunction with a play on words

(Created by Max Maven)

The spectator is asked to think of any word and, using the deck of cards, to spell it by dealing a card to the table for each letter. The mentalist takes the deck and begins to show the spectator cards taken from the top of the deck, asking her to spell her chosen word silently to herself and to remember the card that falls on the last letter. Afterward, the deck is reassembled, and the mentalist spells to the thought-of card.

Step 1

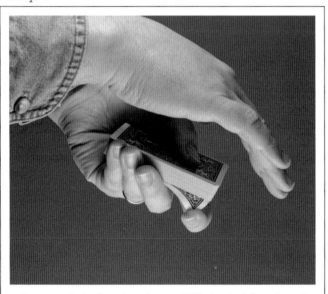

- Borrow a deck of cards and ask the spectator to shuffle it. Take the deck as you say, *"I'm going to ask you to think of a word. It may be any word, in any language, provided you know how to spell it."*

- With the deck face down in dealing position in your left hand, your left first finger reaches to the outer-right corner of the bottom card and pulls downward, bending it. Magicians call this bend in the corner a "crimp." Your right hand hovers above for cover.

Step 2

- Say, *"In order to lock the spelling into your mind, I want you to take the deck and, while my back is turned, spell your word, dealing cards onto the table, one for each letter of the spell. For example, you might be thinking of the word* cat*—and if you are, please say so, and we'll end the experiment* right here. At any rate, if you were thinking of* cat, *you'd deal like this . . ."*

- As you talk, nonchalantly rotate the deck 180 degrees, keeping it face down and flat, so the crimp is now at the inner-left corner near your wrist.

Orson Welles wrote that Max Maven has "the most original mind in magic." Maven's television credits include hosting eight specials in Japan (performing in Japanese) and starring in series in Taiwan, Sweden, Norway, Finland, England, and Canada. Max has been a consultant for most of the top names in contemporary magic and an advisor on over one hundred television shows and is the director of entertainment for the famous Magic Castle in Hollywood. He has published approximately two thousand articles, tricks, and essays, and now he is very tired.

The deck is held this way in the photo only so you can see the crimp and the cards above and below it. In reality the deck is on the table with the crimp at the inner-left corner.

Step 3

Step 4

Gesture toward the deck as you speak.

- Demonstrate by spelling "c-a-t" and dealing three cards one at a time to the table. Drop the balance of the deck on top of the three cards on the table. The crimped card is now fourth from the bottom of the deck.

- Continue: *"When you've finished, drop the rest of the deck on top of your dealt pile, square the cards, and tell me you are ready to go on."*

- Cautioning the spectator to pick up the deck and deal quietly, turn your back.

- At the spectator's indication, face forward and take the deck. *"Now that the spelling is locked into your mind, I'm going to show you cards from this shuffled pack, one at a time. As each card is displayed, I want you to mentally spell your word again, one letter for each card. Please remember the card that falls on the last letter of the spell. Don't stop me when we reach that card—just remember it, and let me keep dealing so that I won't know which one it is."*

117

THOUGHT SPELLER (continued)

The crimp allows you to secretly locate cards that have been lost in the deck. If you crimp the bottom card of the deck, and a chosen card is placed on top and the cards cut, the crimp will now be above the chosen card, making it simple to find. You can cut to it very easily with a little bit of practice. Once the chosen card is below the crimp, you can cut the deck repeatedly or allow the spectator to do so, and the two cards will stay together. Cut the deck—the crimped card goes to the bottom and the chosen card to the top. Place the deck in your pocket and then show your hands empty. Ask the spectator to time you as you try to locate his card *"while the deck is in my pocket."* As fast as you can, jam your hand into your pocket and whip out the top card of the deck. It's a shocker!

Step 5

- Remove the top card of the pack and hold it up so that the spectator can see it.

- Deal the card face down to the table. Continue showing cards, one by one, until ten have been displayed.

Step 6

- At this point ask if the spectator has remembered a card. Because not many spectators will bother to choose a word of more than a few letters in length, the answer will probably be *"Yes."*

- If not, show another five cards. You will then claim to be able to spell *"Your exact chosen word"* to accommodate the extra cards.

Step 7

- The undealt portion of the pack is dropped on top of the dealt pile. Now, as you patter, casually cut at the crimp, transferring all of the cards below the crimp to the top of the deck. The crimp is easily seen at the inner-left corner of the deck—use your right hand to cut the cards, your right thumb at the center of the inner end of the deck so when you cut, you take the crimped card and all the cards above it.

Step 8

The last card will be the spectator's selection, but turn it over slowly to add a little suspense.

- Say, *"You are thinking of a word and a card. I have no way of knowing either. Nevertheless, at this very moment, with no questions asked, I can accurately spell your chosen word and thus arrive at your thought-of card."*

- This is repeated to be absolutely sure that the spectator understands.

- Blithely spell *"y-o-u-r-c-h-o-s-e-n-w-o-r-d,"* dealing one card to the table for each letter of the spell. Ask the spectator to name the thought-of card.

- Turn up the last card dealt. It will be the selection.

WHEN PLANETS ALIGN
Mentalism is about predicting what choices people will make

(Created by Theodore Annemann)

Ask people in the audience to think of the name of a planet in our solar system. After writing a prediction on a piece of paper, fold it in half. Different people call out the names of different planets, and you write each planet that has been mentioned on a different slip of paper, folding each in half and putting it into a small paper bag. One person is allowed to freely pick any one of the folded slips from the bag. After he reads what planet is written on it, your prediction is read aloud, and they match.

Good presentation is the only thing that can make this part of the trick interesting. Try to let your personality sparkle even during dull procedural moments like this.

Step 1

- You need a dark pen, a small pad of paper, and a small bag, like a brown lunch bag or small shopping bag.

Step 2

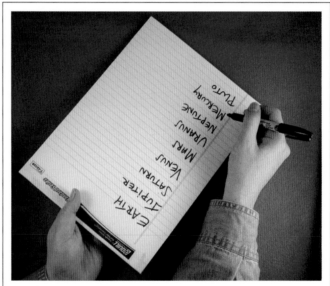

- Write the names of the nine planets on a large pad of paper and point to each one as you mention it when you say, *"Let's see how good your memory is from elementary school: Can you name all nine planets? Earth, Jupiter, Saturn, Venus, Uranus, Pluto, Neptune, Mars, and Mercury. I know there's* been some argument about Pluto, but let's count it for the purposes of our experiment. I am going to predict the future on this piece of paper."

WHO INVENTED THIS?

Theodore (Ted) Annemann was known as the Wizard of Waverly, the town in New York state where he lived. Annemann was a pioneer in the field of "mentalism" and one of its greatest inventors. He published and edited *The Jinx,* a newsletter in the late 1930s and early 40s—it is one of the greatest treasures in all of magic literature. Annemann was also famous for sucessfully performing the infamous Bullet Catch routine. His tragic death by his own hand when he was 35 created a mystique that lasts to this day.

Because the planets have different numbers of letters in their names, you should pretend to write an extra letter or two on some of the slips of paper.

Step 3

- Write "Mars" on one piece of paper without letting anyone see what you've written, then fold it in half and give it to a person to hold—this is your prediction.

Step 4

- Ask someone else to call out the name of any planet. Then, write "Mars" on a piece of paper. This is truly devious: Ignore what the person has said and write "Mars." The people watching will think that you are writing the name of the planet that was called out.

- Fold the paper in half and drop it into the bag.

WHEN PLANETS ALIGN (continued)

You could also call this trick "When Thoughts Align" because that's what is secretly happening: While all the spectators are thinking of different planets, the physical manifestation of their thoughts—your written notes—are all identical. You are forcing their thoughts to align even though they don't know it.

Step 5

- Repeat exactly the same clever thing with everyone else: Each time a planet is called out, write "Mars" on a new piece of paper.

- Each paper is folded in half and dropped into the bag.

Step 6

Just showing you what's on all the papers: They're really all folded and still inside the bag.

- You should have at least five or six different planets chosen. Do all nine if there are enough people. The spectators now think that each piece of paper in the bag has a different planet written on it.

- Actually all of the papers have "Mars" written on them.

Instead of planets you can substitute the names or titles of any other group. For example, you could use colors and make "red" your prediction because you can be assured someone will name it. You could also do it with the names of presidents of the United States and use "Abe Lincoln" as your prediction because he will certainly be among those named if five to nine people are given a choice. If you're at a birthday party, you can have a group of names called out. Use the birthday girl or boy as your prediction because his or her name will certainly be among those named, because it's that person's special day.

Step 7

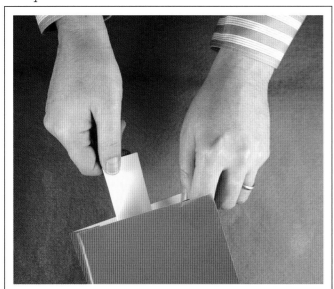

- Ask the person holding the bag, or anyone from the audience, to reach into the bag, mix up the papers, and take out just one.

- As soon as the paper has been removed, take the bag with the rest of the slips inside and crumple it into a ball, then toss it aside, away from the audience.

Step 8

- Close your eyes and ask the person to hand you the slip of paper that has just been removed from the bag.

- Hold it to your forehead. Close your eyes and name the planets slowly, one at a time: *"Earth, Jupiter, Saturn, Venus, Uranus, Pluto, Neptune, Mars, and Mercury.*

The heavenly body written on this piece of paper is . . . Mars. Would you please unfold my prediction and read it aloud?"

- When the spectator reads *"Mars,"* you can bet you'll hear surprised murmurs from the audience.

CELL PHONE DIVINATION

Halfway around the world, someone on the other end of the phone can read the mind of a spectator in your audience

(Created by John Northern Hilliard)

Any card named by a person in the audience is revealed by someone on a cell phone hundreds or even thousands of miles away.

You can introduce this miracle by saying, *"There are those who doubt the ability of the mind to communicate silently over long distances. Let's take a few moments, and together we can prove that thought transference is possible."*

Step 1

	HEARTS	CLUBS	DIAMONDS	SPADES
ACE	Stewart	Dobson	Colt	Hale
TWO	Smith	Darrow	Carver	Harris
THREE	Saks	Driscoll	Campbell	Holmes
FOUR	Sanford	Doogan	Cafferty	Hart
FIVE	Scofield	Dombrowski	Collins	Howard
SIX	Stoddard	Dingle	Cartwright	Hanford
SEVEN	Samson	Draper	Caldwell	Hamlin
EIGHT	Saddler	Dayton	Courtney	Hightower
NINE	Seager	Damato	Cortland	Haskins
TEN	Snyder	Davis	Camp	Hernandez
JACK	Sable	Drake	Craig	Haddon
QUEEN	Sabatini	Dominguez	Cabot	Hedges
KING	Scales	DeLand	Close	Hicks

- Make two photocopies of this chart on card stock and cut them out. In advance, give one copy to a friend who has a cell phone. He is going to be waiting for the spectator to call during your performance.

- You can also scan this chart and e-mail it to someone at the other end of the country or anywhere in the world. The person to whom you give the second copy of the chart will be your secret assistant who will answer his cell phone and apparently read the mind of the spectator standing next to you.

Step 2

- Paper clip the second copy of the chart to the bottom of the second page of a large pad of paper. You also need a marker. Clip the marker to the pad.

- When you are ready to begin the trick, say, *"We are going to have a card thought of, but so you don't think I'm using confederates, we're going to do it in an unusual way. Would someone with a cell phone please hold it up? Good. You, sir—let's use yours. Don't be offended, but would you please leave the room for a moment?"*

WHO INVENTED THIS?

John Northern Hilliard was an old-fashioned newspaper-man in the late 1800s when the telephone first came into common usage. Almost immediately he recognized its potential as a tool for a mind-reading effect. He published this in 1905, and it was immediately stolen and republished by hundreds of magicians and advertising novelty companies who gave it away as a premium on all sorts of paper goods. With the passage of over one hundred years, the idea is again as good as new. The ubiquity of cell phones makes it even more practical, because you can now do it literally anyplace.

Step 3

- Say, "*Just so that nobody believes we have arranged anything in advance, we're going to randomly select a person. Someone please catch this.*"

- While keeping the front of the pad tilted toward you, tear off the first sheet of paper, crush it into a ball, and toss it into the audience.

- To the person who caught the paper ball say, "*Would you please toss that over your shoulder so someone else you don't know can catch it.*" This gives the paper ball to a completely random spectator.

Step 4

- Point to the person holding the paper ball and say, "*Without hesitating, when I count to three, name the value of a playing card: either hearts, clubs, spades, or diamonds. Ready? One, two, three!*"

- Let's say, for example, the person says, "*Diamonds.*" Respond by writing the word "Diamonds" on your pad above the chart.

CELL PHONE DIVINATION (continued)

It's one thing for you to apparently read the mind of someone in the audience, but it's an entirely different and more impressive feat when someone in a distant location seemingly reads the mind of a person standing next to you. Your presentation should play this up—mention how much more difficult it is to read someone's mind over a long distance.

You don't have to use a cell phone, of course—your home phone will work just as well.

Step 4

- Now say, *"When I count to three, name the value of a playing card—ace to ten, jack, queen, or king. Ready? One, two, three!"*

- Let's say the person names *"Seven."* Write "Seven" on your pad. While you are doing that, however, you are looking at the chart. Put the point of your pen on "Seven" at the left side of the chart (the value chosen) and move it to the right until you stop on the third column of names under "Diamond." The name under the tip of your pen is "Caldwell."

Step 5

- Ask the person holding the cell phone to return to the room and say, *"You've been out of the room, and you have no idea what value and suit this person has called out, do you? Good. Will you please dial XXX-XXX-XXXX."* (Here you say the cell phone number of your secret assistant—you can even fold up the first page of the pad and write it on the second page as shown in the photo.) Say, *"Ask for Mr. Caldwell. Then ask him if he knows what card has been thought of."*

126

Adelaide Herrmann was the wife of Alexander Herrmann. She began her career as a dancer and later co-starred with her husband, taking part in his elaborate illusions. After his death in 1896, Adelaide Herrmann continued to present the Herrmann show, first with her nephew Leon Herrmann and then on her own, with a successful vaudeville career. Although there have been few female magicians, Adelaide Herrmann was a notable exception; she combined sleight-of-hand skills with artistic, dramatic, and elaborate illusions, becoming a favorite with audiences. This poster advertises a grisly decapitation effect in which Adelaide appeared to slice off the head of an assistant!

Step 6

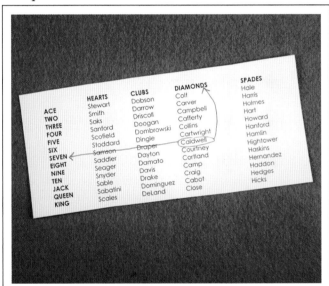

Step 7

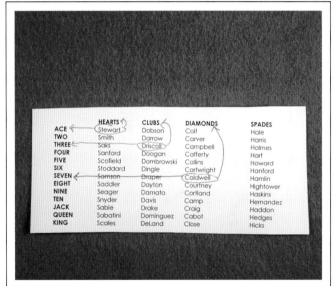

- When the spectator asks for *"Mr. Caldwell,"* your friend on the cell phone immediately does the opposite of what you did based upon the name he is called—he locates "Caldwell" on his chart, then looks at the top of the column to see what suit the card is, then to the left to see its value. The photo indicates what he does, although he doesn't have to make lines on the chart unless he feels it's necessary.

- Your friend replies, *"Yes, I know, the card is the seven of diamonds"* to the person who has called.

- Ask that person to call out the name of the card Mr. Caldwell has announced. Based on the value and suit chosen, you could ask for any of the fifty-two names on the chart to answer the phone—and your buddy will always be able to name the correct card.

- The photo shows how to locate the identities of several other cards based on a different name. For example, Mr. Stewart would be the ace of hearts, while Mrs. Driscoll (if the friend being called is a woman) would be the three of clubs.

PRECURSOR TO DESTINY
Predict a spectator's future with a strip of newsprint

(Created by Albert Spackman)

The magician displays a folded piece of paper on which he has written a prediction. He gives this to a helper from the audience to hold. Next, he holds up a column of text that he has cut from a newspaper. He asks a person from the audience to call "Stop" at any time as he runs a pair of scissors down beside the column of text. When the person stops him at a random spot, the magician snips the column in two. The lower piece flutters to the floor, and the magician asks a person from the audience to pick it up and read aloud the top line at the point where it was cut by the scissors. That line, and the prediction, mysteriously match.

Step 1

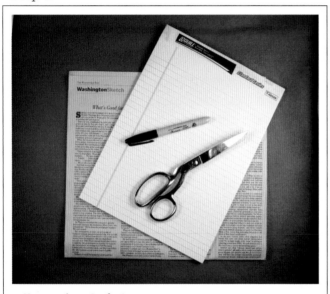

- You need a pair of scissors, a large-size newspaper such as the *New York Times,* a piece of white paper on which to make your prediction, and a marker.

Step 2

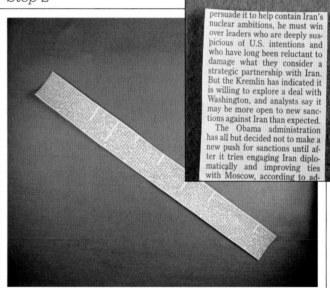

- Cut a 16-inch column of uninterrupted text with no pictures from the newspaper, removing any headline. From a short distance the top and bottom should not be distinguishable from one another—that's the secret. **Remember the top line of the text.**

- Place all of the items onto a table beside you. The newspaper strip should be positioned so that you will grasp the bottom when you pick it up during the performance.

- You should be at least 8 **feet** away from the closest member of the audience.

This trick utilizes a completely different principle than anything else in this book. Put simply, you're holding something too far away from the spectator for him to see it clearly, but the spectator believes he sees it perfectly well. It's an odd thing to explain, but it's based upon a person's expectation that you will hold something right side up. The strip of newspaper is held upside down.

This is one of the few tricks in this book that relies upon your distance from the audience in order for it to work. Before you perform it for a real audience, do a test on a member of your family to make sure you're standing far enough away so that person cannot tell that the strip is upside down.

Step 3

- Begin by saying, *"Newspapers tell you what's happened in the past. I'm going to predict what a piece of newspaper will tell you in the future."*

- Pick up the white paper and make your prediction with the marker—write the top line of text from the newspaper strip that you've remembered. Fold that paper and hand it to a spectator.

Step 4

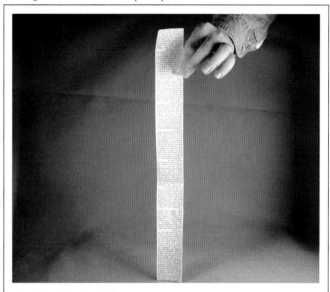

- Pick up the strip of newspaper with your left hand by grabbing its bottom and let it hang straight down. No one will be able to see that it's actually upside down.

129

PRECURSOR TO DESTINY (continued)

In many mental effects, what seems to be a free choice often isn't. Like so many items in magic, it's really a force. In some tricks you need to force a card, in others a color or the name of a planet. Here you are forcing an entire line of text from the top of a strip of newspaper. But, of course, it really doesn't seem possible to an audience that you could do such a thing—not just one word, or one choice, but a line of words.

Step 5

- Your right hand grasps the scissors and positions them, with the blades open and surrounding the newspaper, at the top of the strip.

- Begin slowly moving your right hand downward, the scissors descending along the newspaper strip, and ask the spectator holding the prediction to call out "Stop" at any time.

Step 6

- When you're stopped, your right hand freezes where it is, and you cut the newspaper strip at that point.

A good follow-up to this trick would be to have a second strip of newspaper folded into a small bundle where you could easily pick it up and conceal it in your hand. At the end of this trick, take the two original pieces of newspaper strip and place them on a large plate. Ignite them with a match and allow them to burn until nothing but ash remains. (Make sure there are no hot cinders.) Grasp the ashes with both hands and open up the hidden strip of newspaper as if you've restored it from the ashes.

Step 7

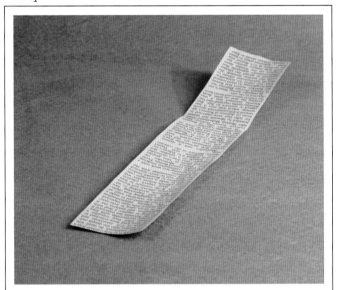

- The portion below the cut will fall to the floor. Quickly place the scissors and remaining part of the strip off to the side.

Step 8

- Pick up the cut-off portion of the newspaper strip— this time from the upper end, so it's right side up. Walk forward to the spectator holding the prediction. Say, *"Please read the top line of the newspaper strip that was cut at the exact point you stopped me, and some- thing I could not possibly have known in advance."*

- After the spectator reads it aloud, ask him to unfold the prediction and read it. The words will match exactly.

PROFESSIONAL SPOON BENDING 1

In real spoon bending, the spoon visually melts apart
at your fingertips

Although the trick Meet Uri Geller in Chapter 8 allows you to appear to bend a spoon, in most professional demonstrations of spoon bending you actually do see a bent spoon. Here's a more advanced version of the trick where the spoon really does bend—then break!

You need two identical spoons that are cheaply made so the metal isn't too thick.

A spoon consists of two parts: the bowl and the handle. Grab the bowl tightly in your left hand and the handle in your right. Bend your hands back and forth until the bowl and handle break apart.

Step 1

The spectators have no idea that one of the spoons is broken—why would they?

- Hold the whole spoon with your left hand between the thumb and fingers. Hold the broken spoon in an identical position in your right hand—your thumb holds both pieces together so the spoon appears to be in one piece.

- You are going to force the spectator to select the secretly broken spoon using the verbal technique called "magician's choice" (also known as "equivoque").

Step 2

- Say, *"Point to either spoon."* If the spectator points to the spoon in your left hand, hand it to him and say, *"You take that one and hold it the same way I'm holding this one."*

- If the spectator points to the spoon in your right hand, say, *"I'll hold that one, and you take the other one. Hold it the same way I do,"* as you give him the spoon from your left hand. The result is the same either way—you always get to keep the prepared spoon that is in your right hand.

The first magician to create a "magical" version of Uri Geller's spoon bending was Dr. Hiroshi Sawa of Japan. From his handling, New York City magician Geoff Latta added the touch of turning the hand sideways and having the spoon slowly "melt" apart, which I've borrowed for this simplified version of the effect. You can get away with the fact that one of the spoons is broken in advance because you seem to allow the spectator to freely choose one spoon—psychologically, if he could have chosen either spoon, then the unspoken conclusion is they both must have been solid to begin with.

Step 3

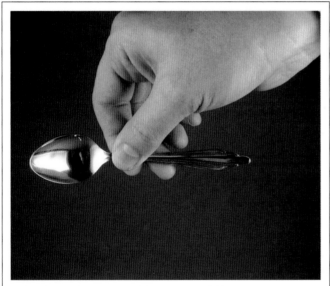

- Hold your right hand beside you and point your fingers downward—your palm is toward the audience.

- Say, *"If I concentrate and use the power of my mind, and your mind, we can cause this spoon to bend."*

Step 4

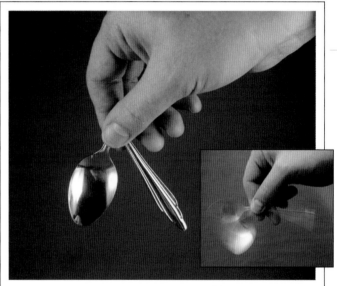

- Take your time—the presentation is the most important part. Encourage the spectators to concentrate.

- After allowing a few moments to pass, slowly (very slowly) relax your thumb's pressure, and the ends of the spoon and handle will naturally bend downward. Do it slowly so the ends creep downward. Allow this to continue until they literally drop from your hand onto the table or floor. Act as if it's real, and you will convince people that it's real.

PROFESSIONAL SPOON BENDING 2
Sometimes "ya gotta have a gimmick"

You're probably wondering if magicians have come up with any cool gimmicks to make a spoon bend—the answer is "yes." The special "something" you need here is so simple you won't believe it. It's a tiny piece of plastic tubing that, when placed onto the ends of a broken spoon, allows it to bend automatically. But it bends with an odd slow motion that gives it an eerie quality.

Step 1

- First, you need a spoon that has had its bowl broken from the handle exactly as in the preceding trick. Next, you need to (using a pliers) bend a small piece of each part—where they would normally join—90 degrees.

- The other thing you need is a piece of flexible, transparent plastic tubing, $3/4$ inch long and $1/8$ inch in diameter.

Step 2

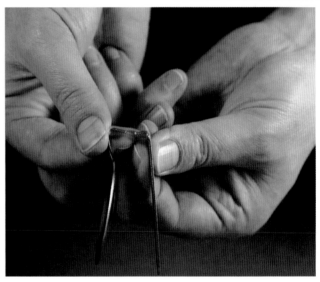

- Squash the plastic tube flat and insert the bent end of each piece of the spoon into opposite ends of the tube.

- The spoon starts bent into a U shape.

If you want to hand the bent spoon out afterward, have an identical spoon that you've really bent in your pocket. After the spoon bends, quickly put it into your pocket and then, as an afterthought, bring out the genuinely bent spoon and toss it on the table.

Step 3

It would be hard to show you this while your hand is in your pocket, so the photo shows it outside the pocket.

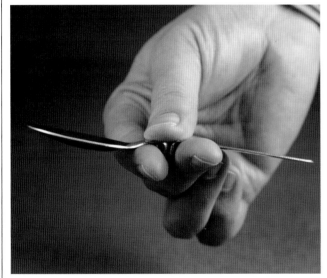

- Have the gimmicked spoon in your pocket before you start. Stick your hand into your pocket and force the spoon open, holding it flat between your thumb and first and second fingers—they keep it from folding. The bent ends with the plastic tubing are con-cealed between your first and second fingers. Your thumb is over the spot where the pieces meet.

- Once the spoon is flat, bring it out of your pocket for display.

Step 4

We're already at step 4, but this is when the trick actually starts from the audience's point of view.

- As with the first method, ask your audience to concentrate really hard on making the spoon bend. The more you put into the presentation, the more con-vincing the trick will be.

- Slowly relax your grip on the spoon, and it will begin to bend in an eerie manner, the plastic tubing forcing the pieces to bend. Make the visible bending last at least thirty seconds, and you'll have a miracle.

TELEKINETIC DISINTEGRATION

A new principle in magic allows a rope to mysteriously melt like butter in your fingers

(Created by Dr. Hiroshi Sawa)

There are many types of rope tricks. Here, however, is something unique in the realm of rope magic—a "psychic" rope trick. A piece of rope is displayed—it appears ordinary. The magician begins to rub a random spot on the rope, and it magically disintegrates. There aren't many mentalism effects using a piece of rope, and this one is unusual, to say the least. Performed with a creepy script in a dimly lit room, it might even scare someone.

The best type of rope for this effect is a thick, soft cotton that can be bought most easily at magic shops.

Step 1

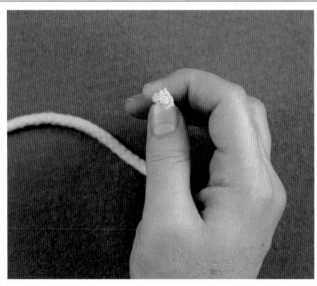

- You need an 18-inch length of braided all-cotton rope. You can find this at your local hardware store.
- Polyester rope is not suitable. The cotton rope must have a core of some sort.

Step 2

- Begin the preparation by rubbing the end of the rope between your thumb and fingers until you can spot the core in the center.

Make sure your incision is neither too long nor too short, and it must be dead center in the middle of the rope.

Step 3

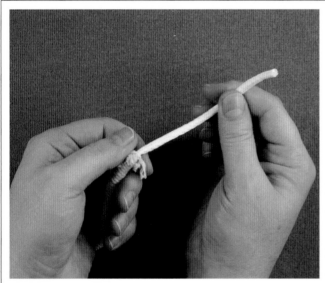

- Pick at the end of the rope until you can grasp the core and pull it completely out. This will leave you with a hollow cotton rope that still looks normal from the exterior.

Step 4

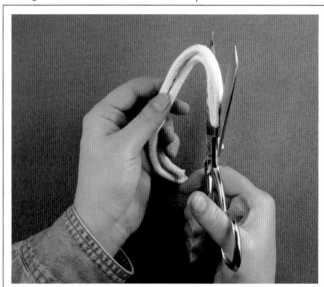

- Fold the rope in half and, using a scissors, cut an incision in its center that's about ½-inch long. Afterward, put the scissors down.

TELEKINETIC DISINTEGRATION (continued)

The real lesson of the new principle utilized for this effect is that even the most ordinary and innocent-appearing object can be altered to allow you to create a miracle. The average person tends to look at things and think that everything that can be done has been done. Creative magicians look at an object and try to discern something about it that can be exploited in a way that is either not obvious to the casual observer or has never been done before.

Step 5

- Gingerly unfold the rope. You can clearly see the place where you cut it.

Step 6

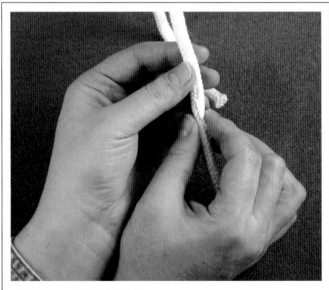

- Using your right first finger and thumb, gently pinch the sides around the slit together to disguise it. You are now ready to perform the trick.

You can add the idea of "choice" to this trick by allowing the spectator to pick the spot where you rub the rope. Do this by asking the spectator to say "Stop" as your right hand descends along the rope. You must time the descent of your hand so that you are stopped at the slit portion of the rope. This is not easy to do without practice, but it is possible to practice and do it well. Watch the corners of the spectator's mouth—they'll start to curl just before she speaks, cuing your right hand to either slightly speed up or slow down.

Step 7

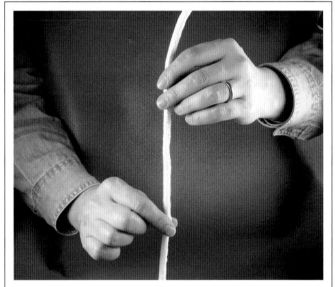

- Your left hand holds the rope by one end so it's hanging freely downward. Say, *"The mind is so powerful that it can both create and destroy."* At the same time, run your right thumb and first finger from the top of the rope down to the point where the incision is. Don't actually touch the rope while doing this.

Step 8

- Begin to very gently rub the cut section of the rope between your right thumb and finger—it will start to disintegrate.

- Move your hand away and allow the audience to see the rope fraying. Rub it a bit more—do it slowly—so it disintegrates further.

- Then move your right hand away and let the spectators see it again. Finally, rub the rope just a bit more, and it will fall into two pieces.

GLORPY

Is it a haunted hankie or your thoughts coming to life?

(Created by Bill Madden and Bernie Trueblood)
This haunted handkerchief trick is one of the most popular props sold in magic shops, but you can easily make it at home with a woman's silk or polyester handkerchief that has a large hem and a piece of wire cut from a clothes hanger.

The result is a prop that does the work for you—it's almost push-button magic. It is nothing short of amazing when you consider that you are creating a haunted handkerchief that seems to have a life of its own while your hands appear to remain perfectly still.

Step 1

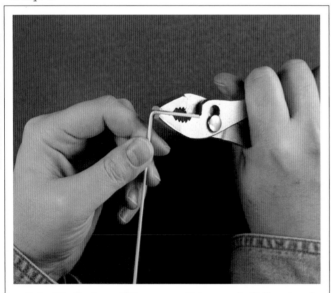

- Cut a 7-inch piece off the straight portion of a thin wire coat hanger.
- Using a pair of pliers, bend 1 inch at a 90-degree angle to the rest to create a "tail."

Step 2

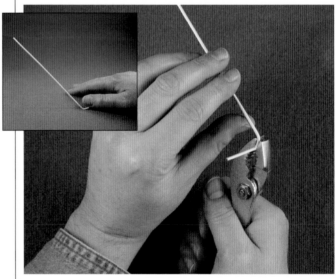

- Here's the most important part: Using the pair of pliers, grasp the long piece of wire just before it curves into the tail and bend it upward.
- If you put the wire onto the table and press downward on the tail with your thumb, the long part will rise. That's the principle on which this miracle is based.

WHO INVENTED THIS?

The basic idea behind this trick is fairly old, but it took two guys working as a company called Madblood Creations (an amalgam of the last names of Bill Madden and Bernie Trueblood) to perfect something that was rarely performed. They added the tiniest improvement by putting a kink in the wire. Instead of having to roll the wire between your fingers, now all you have to do is press down lightly with your thumb. They created one of the most perfect close-up tricks ever invented, only to watch as other companies copied their invention with neither credit nor payment.

Step 3

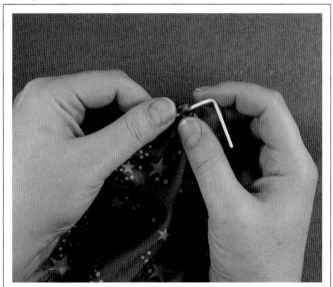

- Poke a small hole in the hem of the handkerchief right at the corner. Slide the long end of the wire all the way into the hem.

- Now you'll have to twist and fidget a bit to get the curved tail of the wire inside and then allow it to slip around the corner. The preparation of the handkerchief is complete:

Step 4

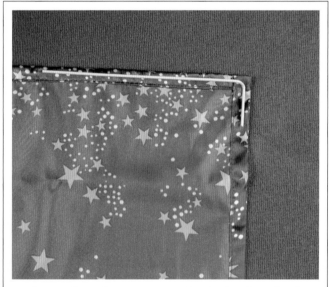

- When you're ready to perform this trick, lay the hanky onto the table so the wire is at the outer-right corner and the kink in the tail makes it go down.

- Note in the photo that the wire is shown outside the hanky solely so you can see its position. The wire is actually inside the hanky's hem and cannot actually be seen.

GLORPY (continued)

Because we're talking about mental mysteries, let's tell the spectators that the power of their minds moves the hanky.

This trick is dependent upon some subtlety and acting. Push downward very lightly with your right thumb at first so the hanky barely moves. It should be just a twitch. Pause for a second, then press down so it moves a little more. Repeat this two or three times, each time encouraging the audience to concentrate more strongly in imagining something appearing under the handkerchief. Eventually, after you cause the "figure" under the hanky to undulate a bit, press completely downward so the wire stands upright. Put your left hand flatly on top of the wire's upper end and make small circles of movement—it appears that whatever is under there is solid. Suddenly raise your left hand and let the wire fall flat. Grasp one corner of the hanky and whip it off the table to reveal nothing under it.

Step 5

- Your right hand folds the outer right corner of the handkerchief diagonally inward and to the left until it is somewhat inward and to the right of the center.

- The little kink in the tail of the wire now curves up— this tells you the gimmick is properly positioned. Note in the photo that the wire is shown outside the hanky solely so you can see its position. The wire is inside the hanky's hem and cannot actually be seen.

Step 6

- Fold the remaining three corners of the hanky inward so you end up with a not-very-neat square.

This stock poster was produced in the early 1900s. Instead of using a specially designed image depicting a particular magician, a stock poster could be purchased in quantity and imprinted with the performer's name. Stock posters are interesting because they give a general sense of magic acts of the period. The tricks depicted are standard ones, with yards of paper ribbon, a glass clock dial, or a rabbit. But the image successfully captures the sort of performer who might have come to a town hall or a holiday party with a suitcase of magic, offering a small show of wonderful surprises, excitement, and marvels.

Step 7

- Turn both hands palm down and lower them onto the sides of the square—your right thumb lands directly on the raised tail of the wire. Say, *"The power of the mind can be strong. If we concentrate together, we can cause solid matter to appear inside this handkerchief. Concentrate . . . really con-* centrate hard and imagine *that there's something solid coming to life inside this handkerchief."*

Step 8

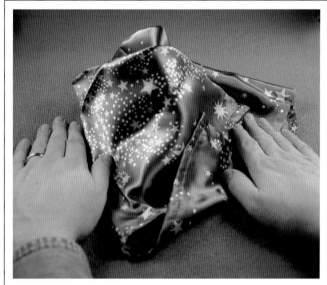

- As you talk, your right thumb pushes down on the curved tail: This will cause the long portion of the wire to pivot upward, and it will appear as if there's "something" inside the hanky.

- Slowly press and release with your thumb several times, sometimes pushing down harder than others to make the center of the hanky undulate at different heights.

- After a few moments, grab a corner of the hanky, quickly lift, and shake it to reveal . . . nothing.

VANISHING ROPE KNOT

It's the easiest way in the world to make a knot vanish

There are many ways to make a knot vanish from a length of rope, including difficult methods involving sleight of hand that require years of practice. This, however, is certainly the simplest. And you'll enjoy doing this because the method is so clever. It does have the advantage of adding a bit of mystery by concealing the rope inside a tube for a moment—and there can never be enough mystery in magic.

Make sure to keep the knot very loose! A tight knot will catch around your finger later on.

Step 1

- You need a cardboard tube: One from an empty roll of paper towels will work. Although you can decorate it, sometimes it's just better to let people see what it really is. It looks less suspicious because it's a familiar object.

- Cut a 1-inch-diameter hole in its center. You also need a piece of rope about 18 inches long. White cotton rope works best.

- Begin by tying a loose knot in the center of the rope. Do not pull it tight!

Step 2

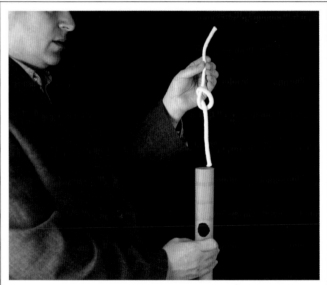

- Lift the tube with your right hand and hold it so the hole is facing you (the audience never sees it) between your thumb and second finger. Your first finger is ready to enter the hole.

- The knotted rope is held above the tube.

144

This may be a simple trick, but here is the moment when you can kill it—avoid drawing attention to the rear of the tube when you look down and insert your finger inside!

Step 3

- Slowly lower the rope straight down into the tube. Watch the hole and, when the knot appears in it, insert your right first finger into one of the loops.

It's extremely important to pull the rope upward slowly. Done too quickly, it will tighten around your right first finger.

Step 4

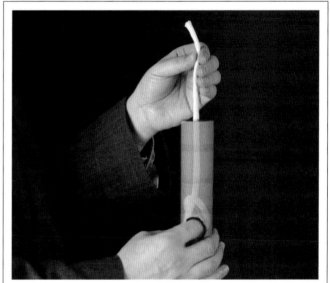

- The cardboard tube is shown as transparent in the photo so you can see the rope inside.

- Your left hand slowly pulls the rope upward, out of the tube. The rope will snake around your right first finger, moving the knot down the rope.

- When the end of the rope snakes past your first finger, the knot will untie. When the rope has been pulled completely out of the tube, the knot will be gone.

SNIP 'N' RESTORE

Few tricks with a rope seem as impossible as a convincing Cut and Restored Rope

Cutting a rope in half, then causing the cut halves to heal so the rope is in one piece, remains one of the most amazing tricks that you can perform—even though magicians have been doing exactly that for many hundreds of years. There is something elemental about the nature of healing that the audience responds to on a deeper level than usual. For this

trick, you'll need a piece of rope at least 3 feet long and a pair of sharp scissors. The last thing you want to do is have the spectator struggle when cutting the rope, so make sure your scissors are up to the task of one quick snip (and handle them carefully).

Step 1

- Put the scissors in your side jacket or trousers pocket to start, point upward.

- Begin with the upper end of the rope held between your left thumb and first finger, about 2 inches below the end. The rope should hang straight down. Note that the rope is held by the center joint of the left thumb, not at the thumb tip.

Step 2

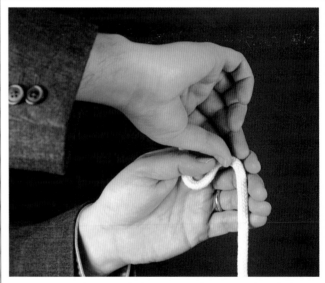

- Say, "*Anyone have a pair of large, sharp scissors?*" That's an odd question, and, of course, no one will have a big pair of scissors in his or her pocket. What the question is really about is psychological misdirection. The audience members have to think about what

you've just said, and while they're doing that . . .

- Your right hand grasps the bit of rope just under your left thumb and pulls it to the right, creating a small loop. Then curl your left fingers slightly to hold the loop in place.

Dante's real name was Harry Jansen, a Swedish-American magician who found success in vaudeville. When American magician Howard Thurston was looking for a business associate, he partnered with Jansen, helped him enlarge his show, and suggested the name Dante. The Dante show toured the world and even appeared on Broadway in the 1940s. A charismatic performer with a twinkle in his eye, Dante performed elaborate, colorful illusions that were arranged in a revue-style show titled "Sim Sala Bim." The charming Dante can be seen performing as himself in the 1942 Laurel and Hardy film *A Haunting We Will Go*.

Step 3

- Look at the audience quizzically and say, *"No?"* (in reference to the scissors). Continue, *"That's okay—I do."* Your right hand brings out the scissors and puts them on the table.

- Say, to a spectator close to you, *"Please pick up the scissors."* Asking the spectator to do something is also a form of misdirection. At that moment, your right hand grasps the center of the rope and raises it straight up until it's behind your left hand for an instant.

Step 4

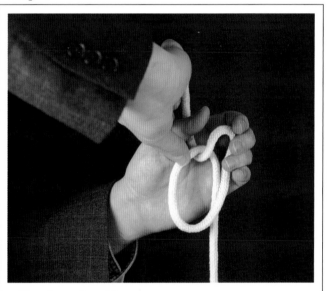

- Place the center of the rope over the loop hidden inside your left hand.

SNIP 'N' RESTORE (continued)

The method explained here is not what you usually read in magic books written for the public (that's you). It's more psychologically advanced. Here's another way to present the restoration. Once the rope has been cut by the spectator, place the scissors aside. Tie the two ends of the short piece (which circles around the center of the long piece) into a single knot. You may then display the rope freely—it looks like two pieces tied together at the center. Ask a spectator to hold one end of the rope while you hold the other. Snap your fingers over the knot and then slide it about 6 inches down the rope: That surprises the spectator because knots generally don't move. Snap your fingers over the knot again and, this time, slide it completely off the end of the rope and toss it away. The rope is restored.

Step 5

- Let go of the rope's center and immediately grasp the hidden loop and pull that up into view above your left first finger—it appears to be the center of the rope.

Step 6

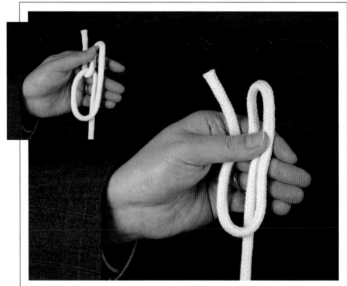

- Straighten the upper end of the rope and the loop beside it, then pull down on the loop and end hanging downward—this puts all the dirty work under your left thumb, and you can turn your left palm toward the spectators and they see what appears to be the center of the rope held between your left thumb and first finger.

- The inset photo shows how it looks if you were to remove your left thumb—but this is only so you understand things more clearly.

Harry Rouclere was an American magician who had a long career at the end of the nineteenth century. Part of his appeal was his virtuosity; he performed magic, juggled, and even exhibited trained dogs. His wife, Mildred, was a singer and dancer, and they formed an act called Mildred and Rouclere, or the Mildred Novelty Company, performing in vaudeville. This poster advertises one of Rouclere's most popular effects, an illusion invented by his friend Servais Le Roy. Mildred was covered with a sheet and then levitated high into the air over the stage. When he pulled away the sheet, she instantly disappeared. How popular is this illusion? It's still performed all around the world every day of the week.

Step 7

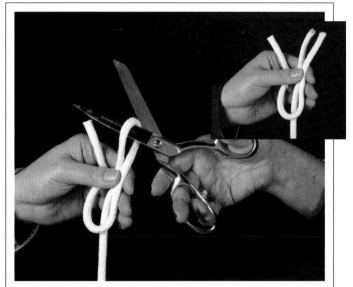

- Ask the spectator to cut *"the center of the rope"* as you point at the loop protruding above your left hand. There is no illusion in all of magic that's more viscerally effective than when the spectator cuts that rope. Allow the long end of the rope just cut to drop straight down. You now have a small U-shaped piece at the top and the long piece (most of the rope) hanging through it.

- Say, *"Please hand me the scissors,"* and take them with your right hand, ready for your own bit of cutting.

Step 8

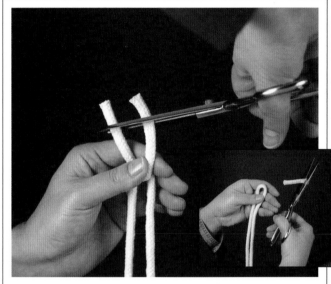

- While being careful you don't cut your left thumb, quickly snip away at the two ends of the short piece, cutting off little bits in about three or four snips.

- There should only be a tiny bit of the short piece remaining. Nip it with the scissors and boldly yank it away, as if it is just another small piece you've cut off.

- Put the scissors down, snap your fingers over your left hand, and then quickly snap the rope out to its full length to reveal the restoration. No one will notice that it's a few inches shorter than at the start!

HYPNOTIC ROPES

This classic routine never fails to mystify an audience

(Created by Bob Carver)

This, one of the most famous of all rope tricks, is still one of the best even though it's well-known. The illusion that three ropes of different lengths become the same length is so strong that even if someone has seen it before, it remains a mystery.

You need three pieces of soft cotton rope. The large piece is 45½ inches long, the medium piece is 26 inches long, and the short piece is 8 inches long. Note that in order for you to be able to see what's happening inside the hands, the photos cannot show the ropes all the way down to the bottom—if we did that, the hands would be too small in the image. So, to keep things clear, the ends of each rope have

Step 1

- Display the three pieces of rope to the audience and let someone examine them.

- Put the pieces into your left hand one at a time so they are held between the thumb and first finger near the upper end. The short piece is placed into position first, then (to the right)

the long piece, and then (farthest to the right) the medium piece.

- Just over 1 inch of each piece of rope should extend upward past your left thumb. The colors of the ends run blue, red, yellow from left to right.

Step 2

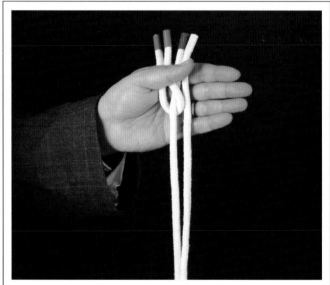

- Your right thumb and fingers reach behind the medium and long pieces to grasp the lower end of the short piece (blue end).

- Raise the lower end of the short piece, wrapping it around the long piece, until it is beside the other end of the short piece.

- Both ends of the short piece, which encircle the long piece, are held by the left thumb. The colors run blue, blue, red, yellow from left to right.

pieces of colored tape around them: blue for the ends of the short rope, red for the ends of the long rope, and yellow for the ends of the medium rope. I suggest you color the ends of your ropes the same way in order to learn the trick. As you follow along with the text and photos, make sure that the colors of the ends of your ropes are in the same positions shown in the photos. Once you've learned the trick, you must do it with all white ropes.

Step 3

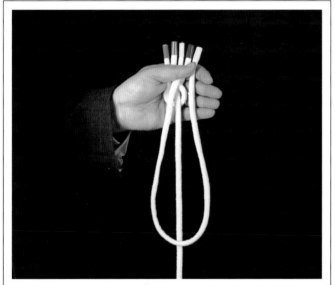

- Your right hand grasps the lower end of the medium piece (yellow) and lifts it. It is placed under your left thumb directly to the right of both ends of the short piece.

- The ends now run blue, blue, yellow, red, yellow from left to right.

Step 4

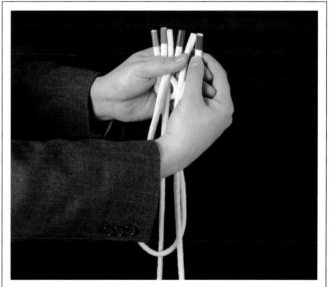

- Your right hand reaches down and grasps the lower end of the long piece (red). It is raised and held, still by the right hand, at the right end of the other five ends held by the left hand.

- The colors run blue, blue, yellow, red, yellow, red.

HYPNOTIC ROPES (continued)

So far you've just set the ropes into position. Here comes the magic.

As you stretch the ropes (your hands moving apart) to the same size, it's important not to do it too quickly. Do not yank your hands apart. There's no chance for the audience to see the ropes appear to visibly change sizes if you do that. Move your hands apart slowly and with effort, as if it takes great strength to pull the ropes into three equal sizes.

Step 5

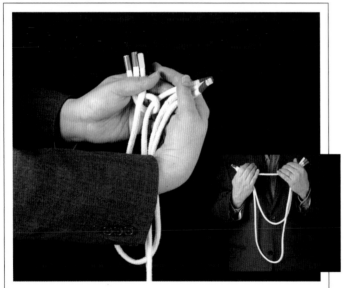

- Your right hand nips the three ends on the right (red, yellow, red) between the thumb and first finger and begins to pull them to the right. At the same time, your left hand pulls the other three ends (blue, blue, yellow) to the left.

- The long rope will slide through the short rope as the hands separate, creating the illusion that the short rope is being stretched and the long rope is simultaneously shrinking.

- The inset photo is an audience view just as you start to pull your hands apart.

Step 6 Don't rush this part because it's the magical moment in the effect.

- Pull your hands as far apart as you can until the ropes stop you.

- Your right hand releases the ends it holds one end at a time, and they swing downward. The stretching illusion is now completed, and all three ropes appear to be the same size.

152

Robert Carver was a magician from Georgia who one day saw another magician with the extremely unusual name of "Hen" Fetsch perform a rope trick. He was impressed with some of Hen's unusual ideas, and Carver went on to create The Professor's Nightmare, for which he won the International Brotherhood of Magicians Originality Trophy in 1957. The name of the trick changes based upon the patter you use. Here, I've chosen Hypnotic Ropes as a slightly different patter theme.

Step 7

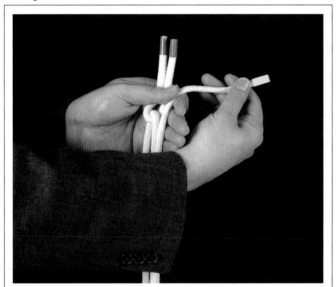

- You will now apparently count the three ropes one at a time, seeming to prove that they are separate from one another. Briefly, this is accomplished by counting the medium rope first on *"one,"* then switching it for the combined short/long ropes on *"two,"* then taking the medium rope a second time on *"three."*

- Here's how. Grasp the medium rope (yellow) between your right thumb and first and second fingers 1 inch or so from its upper end and pull it away from your left hand. Count, *"One."*

Step 8

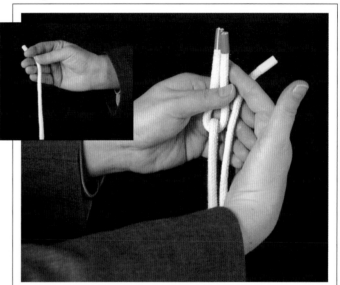

- Clip the yellow end of the medium rope between your right first and second fingertips, freeing your thumb.

- Bring your right hand back to your left hand so the medium rope lies on your left fingertips, and your right first fingertip is behind the blue ends of the short rope.

HYPNOTIC ROPES (continued)

Here is where you'll prove that all three ropes are the same size—the most difficult part of the routine. The false count described on this page is not easy to do, and it's important because it reinforces the illusion that the three ropes are both separate and the same length. Without the false count,

it's only half a trick. So practice the false count until you can switch the ropes smoothly and without breaking rhythm. Count *"One, two, three"* slowly and make sure your hands follow the count.

Step 9

- Move your right thumb onto the blue ends of the short rope, pressing them against your right first finger. Also, move your left thumb onto the medium piece of rope (yellow) 1 or 2 inches lower down, pressing it against your left fingers.

- Move your right hand, holding both blue ends of the short rope, upward. Count, *"Two."* The medium rope remains in the left hand. The folded-over portions of the short and long ropes are concealed inside your right fingers.

Step 10

- Move your right hand upward and to the right until the lower red ends of the long rope clear the left hand and swing freely.

- Your right hand returns to your left hand and, while continuing to hold the two ropes, also takes the medium rope beside them.

Pull the medium rope out of your left hand as you count, *"Three."*

- All three ropes of apparently equal size appear completely separate.

This is the weakest part of the trick. If you were going to magically cause the ropes to return to their original sizes, it wouldn't be by just bunching all of them into your hand and then pulling them out again. However, this is the easiest way to end it and it has worked for thousands of magicians for decades. Good presentation really counts here. Make it mysterious.

Step 11

- Return the ropes to your left hand, holding the upper ends between the left thumb and first finger as they were before the count. Your right hand now brings the three lower ends upward, also placing them beneath the left thumb.

- Wave your right hand magically over your left hand. Grasp a red end with your right hand and pull it upward, pulling the long rope completely free of the others.

You can really pull the ropes free in any order to reveal that they've returned to their original sizes.

Step 12

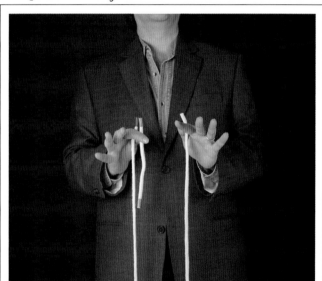

- Grasp a blue end and pull the short rope free. Your left hand displays the remaining rope (medium) by allowing one end to drop, and all three pieces are seen to have returned to their original sizes.

- After you have practiced and learned the trick, remove the colored tapes from the ends of the rope and practice again until you can tell which end is which and where they go even without the colors—then you'll be able to perform it for an audience.

OLD ABE WAS A MOODY MAN
This simple yet delightful trick uses a piece of paper currency

(Created by Bob Read)

Some years ago a clever (and unknown) person discovered that by making three straight folds in a piece of paper money, the portrait can appear to change expressions, smiling and frowning, as the bill is turned at various angles to the eye.

This is a hilarious and intriguing illusion, but it is obvious just how the bill is being manipulated. The late Bob Read, who was England's finest comedy magician, managed, through a sublimely simple handling, to conceal the fact that the angle at which the bill is being viewed is purposely changed.

Step 1

- Take a new $5 bill that is fairly clean and fold it in half, vertically bisecting Abe's right eye.
- Sharply crease the fold. (This is known as a "mountain fold" in the world of origami.)

Step 2

- Open the first fold and make a second, identical mountain fold through Abe's left eye. Crease it.

WHO INVENTED THIS?

Bob Read was the funniest and most amazing stand-up magician in England's history. His hilarious patter lines were the perfect example of how humor is the best misdirection. He was particularly well-known for being able to produce a full bottle of champagne from underneath an apparently empty handkerchief right under your nose. His misdirection? A really bizarre fake nose that, when he removed it, hid another fake nose beneath. He compounded the hilarity by saying, "That's not my real nose ... that's my real nose," as he pulled off the first fake nose to reveal the second. I think he could have produced an elephant at that moment. A beloved magician all over the world, he was also an author and collector of ancient prints depicting magicians and a historian of magic and its quirky past.

Step 3

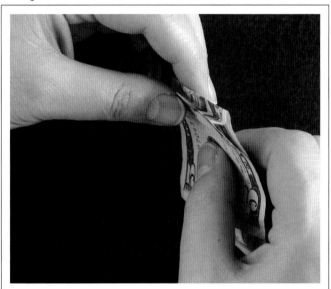

- Bring those two folded edges together, making a "valley fold"—the opposite of a mountain fold because the center of the fold goes downward—between them. Crease it.

Step 4

- Open the bill out flatly, allowing some of the ridges of the two mountain folds to rise. This distorts the portrait when it is looked at on an angle: Tilting the upper edge of the bill away from you will cause Abe to smile (upper photo), while tilting the upper edge toward you will cause him to frown (lower photo).

- Any light must fall onto the face of the bill.

OLD ABE WAS A MOODY MAN (continued)

Here is Bob Read's improvement to the classic effect, so you don't have to openly turn your hands as much.

Also note that you don't have to prepare the bill in advance. If you're good at small talk, you can borrow a bill and make the three required folds while you carry on a conversation.

The trick is even more amazing this way, and you return the bill to the spectator at the end. That way she gets to keep a great souvenir of your performance, and she might, if she has the nerve, even show it to her friends.

Step 5

- Fold the bill in half just to the left of Abe's head.

Step 6

Hold your right hand off to your right side with Lincoln's portrait facing directly toward the spectator.

- Your right hand grips the bill at the right end between the thumb, on the front, and the fingertips, on the back.

John Nevil Maskelyne was one of England's greatest magicians and a showman, entrepreneur, and inventor who established many trends for Victorian magicians. His theaters in London, Egyptian Hall and St. George's Hall, became laboratories for great magic. Maskelyne's inventions included a trunk escape, a mechanical man who seemed to think and play cards, and a perfected method for levitating a human being. John Nevil Maskelyne developed dozens of innovative magical creations. One of Maskelyne's favorite themes was spirit séances; this poster advertises one of Maskelyne's illusions in which a glowing skeleton appeared on stage.

Step 7

- With a slight shake of the right hand at the wrist, your thumb shoves the front half of the bill upward a tiny bit, causing it to buckle slightly. This, combined with the tiniest tilt (just a few degrees) of the wrist, causes Abe to smile.

Step 8

- Shake your right hand at the wrist a second time and pull downward on the front half of the bill with your right thumb, buckling the paper in the opposite direction. Also, tilt your right hand downward just a bit—old Abe will make a big frown.

BUDDHA BILLS

An ancient principle is updated for performance out of your pocket

The Buddha Papers was first described in English by Reginald Scot in his book *The Discoverie of Witchcraft* in 1584—the first book in English to explain detailed conjuring methods. Although the trick is well-known among magicians, it is little used today, although you'll find it to be simple to construct and perform—and it will fool every person for whom you do it. Instead of using colored papers, I've created a version using paper currency—a much more natural and adult item for you to hold.

If you can use $100 and $50 bills here, the trick will seem more impossible because people are less likely to suspect them of trickery.

Step 1

- You need four bills: You can use two each of any denomination, but the higher the value of the bills, the less likely anyone will think that you've done anything unusual to them. Let's assume you have two $20 bills and two $5 bills. (If all you have available are fives and ones, the trick will still work.) The two fives must be identical, as must the two twenties—in other words, don't mix old-style and new-style currency.

Step 2

- Place one $5 bill squarely on top of one $20 bill, both portrait side up and right side up. Now fold over the right third of the $5 bill.
- Fold over the left third of the $5 bill.

With a bit of folding and pasting, you are going to create a simple gimmick that will secretly exchange one thing for another. Make sure you have a glue stick ready.

Step 3

Try to make both sets of folded bills look as similar as possible.

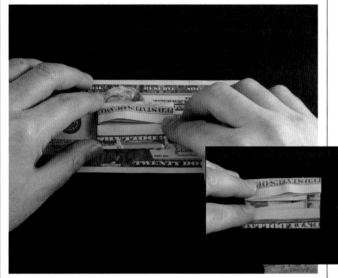

- Fold the top and bottom of the $5 bill toward the center. Once the $5 bill has been folded, fold the $20 bill over it in exactly the same series of steps (right third over, left third over, top and bottom to center).

- Do exactly the same thing with the second set of bills.

Step 4

Use a stack of very heavy books so the glued-together bills are as flat as a pancake after a day or two.

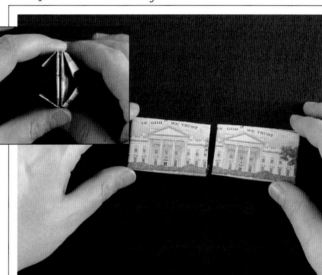

- Turn both sets of folded bills over so what remains of the backs of the $20 bills is visible.

- Using the glue stick, paste the two sets of folded bills back to back (see inset photo). Once that's done, place them under a bunch of heavy books overnight until they've been flattened.

BUDDHA BILLS (continued)

By using paper currency for this trick, there is little suspicion focused on the props. And while I'm explaining how to magically turn two quarters into five dimes here, the Buddha Bills can be used to exchange any two objects. For example, you can write the name of a card on a piece of paper and fold it up in one side of the gimmicked bills. Display an identical blank piece of paper and openly fold it up in the $5 bill, which is then folded inside the $20 bill. Force the same card (whose name you've written in advance) as explained in chapter 3. Secretly turn the bills over and unfold them to reveal that the previously blank piece of paper now has the name of the "freely" chosen card written on it.

Step 5

- The gimmick is now finished, and it appears identical on both sides. If you unfold the $20 bill on either side, there will be a folded $5 bill inside it. Unfold the $5 bill on the side you've opened and place five dimes inside it. Refold the $5 bill, then fold the $20 bill around it.

- Turn the whole thing over so the empty bills are uppermost, and you're ready to begin.

Step 6

- Bring the prepared packet out and hold it in your left hand, with the slight bulge created on the underside by the duplicate set of folded bills nestled in your second and third fingers. This keeps them from being seen by the audience.

Step 7

While we're changing coins in this case, any small flat object can be magically transformed using the gimmicked bills.

- Unfold the upper $20 bill, then unfold the $5 bill inside it. Ask for two quarters and have them placed on the center of the $5 bill. Refold the $5 bill, then the $20 bill. The quarters are trapped inside.

- Your right hand rotates the right end of the folded bills counterclockwise until it faces away from you, as in the inset photo.

Step 8

This clever way of secretly turning something over, by pushing it through the fist, was invented by Dai Vernon and is called, appropriately, the Through-the-Fist Flourish.

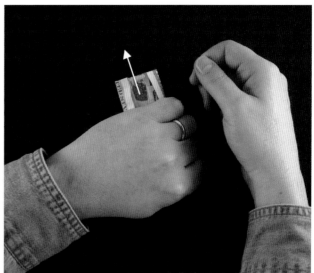

- Close your left hand around the folded bills, then turn your fist palm down.

- Use your left thumb to push the bills out the pinky side of your fist—done in a magical gesture that secretly turns the packet over.

- Grasp it with your right hand and pull it away from your left hand. Turn your left hand palm up, then lower the bills into it so the bulge is again nestled by the second and third fingers. Unfold the $20 bill, then the $5 bill, to reveal the five dimes. Spill them onto the table or the spectator's hand.

MR. JACKSON TAKES A POWDER

This visible change from one bill to another is not easy, but it's good

(Created by Nicholas Night)

Buried in a magazine I published decades ago is one of the most original effects with a bill ever created. You display a folded $20 bill and ask the spectator to initial it. Then you hold the bill between your hands, and it instantly changes into a $5 bill—which still has the spectator's initials on it!

Step 1

- You need a $5 bill, a $20 bill, a pair of small scissors, and a paper clip.

- Cut out Andrew Jackson's portrait from the $20 bill. Make sure to follow the outline of his hair as neatly as you can and note where the cut on his left shoulder ends in the inset photo.

Step 2

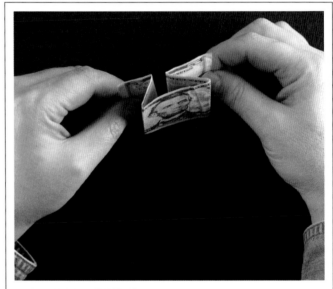

- One at a time, fold both sides of the $5 bill behind and then forward again in a Z pattern. The vertical fold on the left is made just to the left of Lincoln's ear, while the fold on the right is made on the right edge of the "T" in "The," to the right of his head.

For over twenty years Nicholas Night and his wife Kinga combined "the art of magic with the magic of art" on television and stages around the world with one of the most unique illusion acts ever created. Set in a theatrical artist's studio, Night's act brought his creations to life with such signature illusions as Spray Paint and Garbage Guy. Today he brings art to life literally, working as an animation executive and creator in Los Angeles.

Step 3

- When the $5 bill is pressed flat, the only thing that identifies its value is Lincoln's face.

Step 4

When Jackson's head is properly aligned over Lincoln's you will appear to have a folded $20 bill.

- Place the cut-out head of Jackson over Lincoln, neatly lining up the bottoms. You'll find that a little "tail" of Jackson's shoulder (on your left side) will extend past the edge of the folded $5 bill—tuck it around the fold, as shown in the inset photo.

BILL TRICKS

MR. JACKSON TAKES A POWDER (continued)

This is one of the more difficult tricks in the book. The set-up isn't easy—it may take you a few tries to cut out Andrew Jackson's head properly. Positioning it over Lincoln's head precisely requires patience. Handling the set-up bill requires care; you don't want Jackson's head to accidentally move. When you rest the bill on the table for the spectator to initial it, you've got to press downward in just the right way to keep the edges of Jackson's head from flaring up. Then, of course, there's the end, where you must conceal the cut-out of Jackson's head in your left fingers. Yes, this one is going to take some practice.

Step 5

- Slide the paper clip onto the front portion of the folded $5 bill (larger portion of the clip on the front) so that it encircles Jackson's eyes. Note that the paper clip does not go completely around both folded edges of the $5—just the front fold.

- Place the set-up bill into someplace like your wallet, where it will be kept flat.

Step 6

This is when the trick starts for the spectators.

- To perform the trick, bring the set-up bill out of your wallet and turn its face away from you. Grasp its left end with your left hand, fingers in front and thumb behind.

- Turn your left hand palm down and lower it to the table, pressing downward enough to keep the right end of the folded bill (and the side of Jackson's cut-out head) pressed on the table. Ask the spectator to write his initials just above Jackson's shoulder—point to the spot with your right first finger, as shown in the inset photo.

Note, in the inset photo, how your left second, third, and fourth fingers are already covering a good part of Jackson's portrait.

The most amazing part is when the spectator sees that his initials are still on the bill after the change.

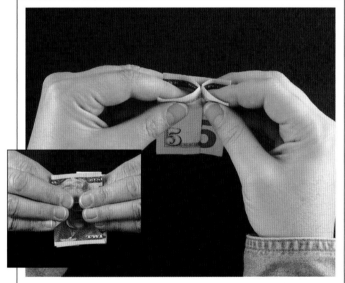

- Now raise the bill so the portrait is facing the audience. Grasp both ends in an identical way: Your thumbs and first fingers clip the innermost folded flaps near the top—your first fingertips are actually inside the folds.

- The inset photo shows how this appears to the audience.

- Quickly extend your left fingers over Jackson's portrait and rapidly pull your hands apart until the $5 bill is stretched flat between them. The paper clip will remain on the cut-out of Jackson's head as your left fingers pull it inside them. The spectators suddenly see Lincoln where Jackson was a moment earlier.

- Your right hand pulls the bill free of your left hand and places it on the table. Point out that the spectator's initials are still on it. Your left hand falls to your side with the extra piece—get rid of it in your pocket.

THE IRON TOOTHPICK
It's so simple a child could do it, yet this trick remains worthy of performance by anyone

This is the easiest of tricks, which anyone can do, yet it is very potent for a simple reason: The spectator is involved in a hands-on way. There are many tricks where things are broken, ripped, burnt, and so on, only to be restored. This is one of few I can think of where the spectator does the destroying—here s/he breaks the toothpick in half. The tactile nature of that moment is extremely strong and convincing. The toothpick is restored to its unbroken state at the end.

Step 1

- You need a supply of wooden toothpicks and a handkerchief or scarf with a ¼-inch hem.

Step 2

- Use a small scissors to open the stitches on one end of the hanky and slide one of the toothpicks inside the hem.

THE ART OF MAGIC

Chung Ling Soo was the stage name of an American magician, William Ellsworth Robinson. Robinson was a creative magician who worked as an assistant to Harry Kellar and Alexander Herrmann. But he had little success as a performer. Once he began impersonating a Chinese magician, he became a star on the music hall stage in England in the early years of the twentieth century. Chung Ling Soo presented an elaborate show; his magic was artistic and colorful, and his advertising was equally flamboyant, befitting his role of an Asian master of magic.

Step 3

- Place another toothpick on the center of the open handkerchief and fold the corners of the hanky over it.

Step 4

- Begin the performance by unfolding the handkerchief to reveal the toothpick, which you pick up and display. Say, *"This toothpick is made of iron. I know ... it looks like an ordinary wooden toothpick—but it's not."*

THE IRON TOOTHPICK (continued)

Although this is an easy trick to do, every trick requires careful thought when performed. The potential trouble spot here is when you pick up the toothpick through the cloth. It's possible to accidentally pick up the wrong toothpick—the one in the middle rather than the one in the hem. You won't be able to tell the difference through the cloth, and if you pick up the wrong one, and the spectator breaks it, there is no way to successfully finish the trick. There is no embarrassment greater than not being able to bring a trick to a proper conclusion. So, be very careful and follow the instructions precisely.

Do not fold the hem containing the extra toothpick directly on top of the whole toothpick!

Step 5

- Place the toothpick back onto the center of the handkerchief.

- Select a spectator and ask her to come closer.

- Fold the corner of the handkerchief that contains the duplicate toothpick in the hem over the center

- of the hanky, then past it, closer to you. The duplicate toothpick in the hem is now closer to you than the regular toothpick—remember that!

- Fold the other three corners of the handkerchief to the center.

Step 6

- Feel through the cloth and locate the duplicate toothpick in the hem—it's the one closer to you.

- Say, *"No matter how hard you try, you will not be able to break the toothpick."*

This is, perhaps, the easiest trick in this book. Although it's been explained many times before, few people have actually seen it performed, and there's ample opportunity for byplay when the spectator unexpectedly cracks the toothpick in half. She might stop as she feels it start to bend, and you'll have to coax her to complete the break. Insist that it's made of iron and can't be broken. That bit of patter creates some dramatic tension, then comedy, when it does break.

This part is critical! Watch that you pick up the correct toothpick, or else the trick will fail.

Step 7

- Ask the spectator to grasp the toothpick through the cloth (hold it until she takes it). Tell her to go ahead and try to break it—*"It's impossible."*

- There will be a distinct "crack" as she snaps the toothpick in half. Say, *"Oops! It's not supposed to do that. Uh ... Let's use some magic to fix it. Please let go of the handkerchief."*

Step 8

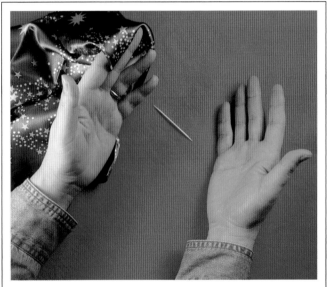

- Wave your hand over the handkerchief, then slowly unfold it to reveal the whole toothpick in the center, lifting it by the corners so the whole toothpick falls to the table (this silently proves that there are no broken pieces from another toothpick just lying in the hanky).

- Remove the toothpick and hand it to the spectator as a souvenir. Fold the handkerchief and put it into your pocket.

- Later on, remove the broken toothpick from the hem and replace it with a fresh one.

THROUGH THE TABLE

Here's the best trick for an impromptu performance over dinner or at a restaurant

When people know you do magic, they usually don't hesitate to ask you to perform a trick. This often happens when you're at someone's house for dinner or in a restaurant. There are few tricks better than this one for such an occasion.

You borrow a coin and place it onto the table, heads side up. Then you pick up a salt shaker (or a drinking glass) and wrap it in a napkin. You use the napkin because, you explain, a hole will open in the table allowing the coin to pass through, and the sight is so amazing that it drives people crazy. The napkin will prevent anyone from seeing the hole and falling into a deep psychosis. The coin is covered by the wrapped salt shaker but fails to go through the table. You realize that

Step 1

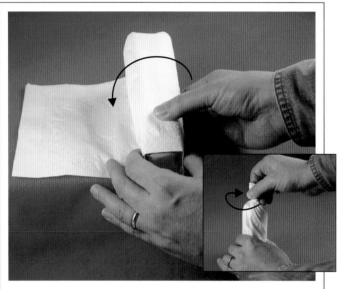

- Place a quarter on the table about 12 inches from your edge, heads side up.

- Open the paper napkin, leaving it folded once, and lay the shaker on it. Roll the shaker inside the napkin, not too tightly, keeping its bottom edge in line with the bottom of the napkin.

- Turn it upright, so the bottom rests on the table, and twist the top of the napkin (see inset photo). If you were to lightly lift the napkin, the salt shaker should stay on the table (don't actually do that, though).

Step 2

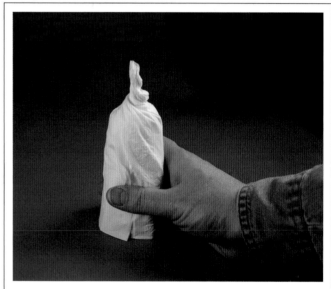

- Grasp the shaker with your right hand, squeezing it just enough to keep it inside the napkin.

- Place it over the coin.

the coin needs to be tails side up, and you turn it over, then cover it again.

Placing both your hands over the wrapped salt shaker, you ask the spectator to place her hands on top of yours. Suddenly, and without warning, you pull your hands out from under hers, then push her hands downward on the salt shaker. The paper napkin crumples flatly to the table—the shake shaker has vanished! It, rather than the coin, has penetrated the table.

It is perfectly natural to pull your right hand, holding the salt shaker, out of the way due to your surprise at seeing the coin still there.

Step 3

- Snap your fingers, then lift the shaker to reveal that the coin is still there.
- Act surprised to see the coin, saying, *"That's odd."*

Step 4

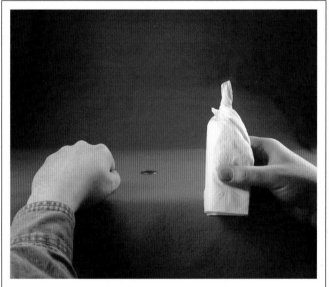

- Retract your right hand to just beyond the table edge and slightly—a hair—below it.
- Pay no attention to the salt shaker.

173

THROUGH THE TABLE (continued)

Of all the items in this book, this trick is perhaps the best example of what magicians call "physical misdirection" (as opposed to "psychological misdirection"). Here, your left hand turning the coin over on the table literally draws the eyes of the spectators to it, and they never see your right hand go near the edge of the table.

Of course, although this is physical misdirection, it was conceived through the use of psychology: Someone had to figure out that you need to have something on the table that people would find of interest—the coin, in this case. People always look at money . . . go figure.

Step 5

- At the same time that your right hand is moving inward, your left hand is moving outward. Say, *"Ah! The quarter has to be heads side up."* Your left hand turns the quarter over. At the same time, allow the salt shaker to drop into your lap while continuing to hold the napkin "shell." Your right hand must remain frozen still when the shaker leaves the shell.

Step 6

- Immediately move your right hand forward and cover the quarter with the napkin shell.
- If you've made the shell properly (neither too tight nor too loose), then it will stand upright over the coin.

Chevalier Ernest Thorn was an inventive Polish magician who toured around the world. Among many of his innovations, one of the most notable is his original cremation illusion, in which his assistant seemed to vanish in flames as she stood within an asbestos curtain. Another was Noah's Ark, in which a pretty model of the ark was shown empty, then opened to show various animals, climaxing by producing a pretty assistant, supposedly Noah's wife! Although he is little remembered today, Thorn's artistic act, called "An Hour in Dreamland," introduced a number of important creations, and he was highly regarded by a generation of important magicians.

Step 7

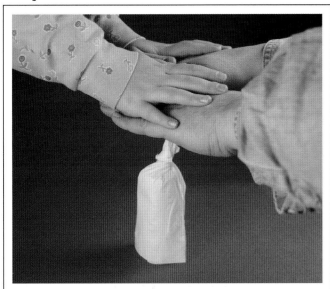

- Hold your palm-down hands just above the napkin.

- Ask the spectator to put her hands on top of yours.

Step 8

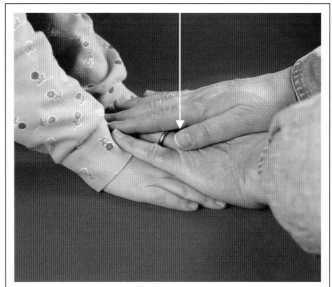

- Quickly pull your hands out and immediately lower them on top of her hands. Before she has a chance to do anything, push her hands downward so they crush the napkin shell flatly onto the table.

- Raise your hands and show them empty. Lift the flattened napkin as if you're not sure what's happened. End by reaching under the table and bringing out the salt shaker.

CUT & RESTORED NAPKIN
There are many methods for this trick, but this is the best, requiring only one napkin and no folding

When working in an impromptu situation, in someone's home or a restaurant, sometimes it's better to cut and restore something you can pick up from the table, like a paper napkin. In these sorts of situations, where you think paper napkins will be around, you should prepare the gimmick at home in advance and just carry it in your pocket.

A good deal of playing the part of a magician is being prepared for different contingencies so you can perform tricks depending upon the circumstance in which you find yourself. Just like a gunfighter, you don't want to leave home with an empty holster.

Step 1

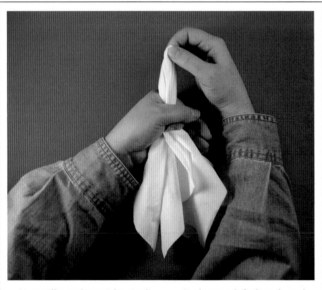

- You will need two identical paper napkins, Scotch tape, and a pair of scissors.

- Begin the preparation by opening a large paper napkin flatly on the table. Grasp the center with your right thumb and first finger and lift it slightly.

- Circle your left thumb and first finger around the part you've lifted and pull it upward until about 2½ inches extend above your left thumb.

Step 2

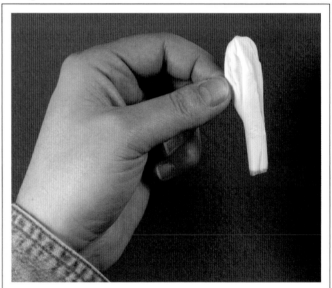

- Cut off this piece using the scissors, then wrap the bottom tightly with the Scotch tape. The gimmick is now complete. Place the gimmick and scissors into your right jacket pocket. (If you're not wearing a jacket, then have them on the seat next to you, with the gim-

mick tucked under your leg, or you might have them in a small briefcase, purse, or bag of some sort and retrieve them from there.)

Step 3

- Begin the performance by opening up a new paper napkin and displaying it, open flat, on both sides. Grasp the center between your right thumb and first finger and draw it upward into your left fist. The tip of the napkin should just extend above the upper side of your fist and be visible to the audience.

Step 4

The secret to a deceptive thumb palm is keeping your thumb relaxed and not pressing it tightly against the side of your hand.

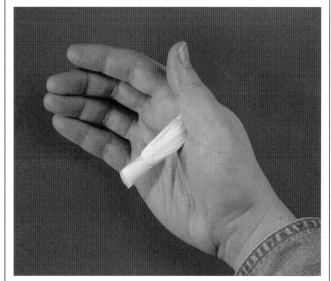

- Say, *"We're going to need a scissors for this,"* as your right hand goes into your pocket. While your hand is out of sight, secretly grip the gimmick in what magicians call a "thumb palm." This is the simplest of all ways to palm something. Simply nip the upper (non-taped) end of the gimmick in your right thumb crotch. Now grasp the scissors, bring them out, and put them onto the table, all the while keeping your right hand palm down.

177

CUT & RESTORED NAPKIN (continued)

Like all tricks, this one has moments that are vital to its success. Here, these are when you add the gimmick to your left hand and when you later steal it back with your right hand. In both cases, your right hand must cover the top of your left fist for a moment in what could, if it's not done properly, seem like an unnatural gesture. Your goal is to decrease the importance of these two moments for the audience—so don't stare at your hands when you do them! Look at the spectator and say something in both instances. Engaging spectators in conversation requires them to think, and when they have to think, they stop watching for a second. Also, don't fumble when you add or steal the gimmick. The subsequent action of your right hand—stroking and pulling the napkin upward—gives you a perfect reason to bring your hands together. Do it smoothly and all will be well.

Step 5

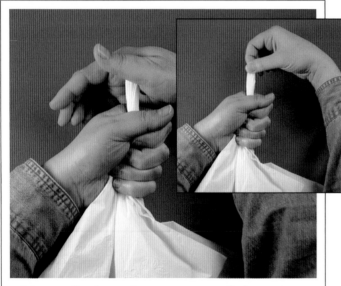

- Bring your hands together directly in front of you and nip the lower (taped) end of the gimmick with your left thumb.

- Immediately draw your right hand straight up, as if pulling the tip of the napkin that was poking out of your left first upward. What you are actually doing is letting your thumb and fingers slide along the gimmick so it appears that you have pulled the tip of the napkin upward for easy access and greater visibility (inset photo).

Step 6

- Using the scissors, your right hand cuts off two or three small pieces from the upper end of the gimmick.

- Afterward, put the scissors down.

The way magicians used to perform this trick was with a white cotton handkerchief borrowed from a spectator instead of a paper napkin. And, rather than using a scissors to mutilate it, the center portion was lit and allowed to burn for a moment before the flame was blown out, then quickly patted by the right hand—and what was left of the gimmick stolen at that moment. These days, it is unlikely that you will be able to borrow a plain white cotton handkerchief, and so using a paper napkin is better. While you can burn the gimmicked part of the napkin instead of cutting it, the paper ignites more rapidly than cloth and it's a bit more dangerous. It's difficult to do magic if you get burned, so leave that for the professionals.

Step 7

- You're now going to reverse the action you performed initially to add the gimmick to the top of your left fist, this time to steal it.

- Bring your hands together in front of you and nip the upper end of what remains of the gimmick in thumb palm in the right hand.

Step 8

- Immediately grip the tip of the whole napkin between your thumb and fingers and draw it upward through your left fist. Let go with your left hand, then give the napkin a good downward shake with your right hand.

- Open the napkin out fully between your hands to reveal that the center is fully restored. As you crumple it up afterward, add the little piece from the thumb palm into the napkin and toss the whole thing away.

HANDKERCHIEF & NAPKINS

IN THE BERMUDA TRIANGLE

This is an oddly baffling and offbeat effect

(Created by Jim Steinmeyer)
This is a very effective impromptu trick and can easily intrigue a group of a dozen people. Where did this come from? Doug Henning saw a child on the streets of India perform a version, and when he returned to America he showed it to Jim Steinmeyer, who was working with him at the time. Jim created

the specific presentation and handling you're about to read.

The performer demonstrates the secret of the Bermuda Triangle, constructing a model of it on the floor. One by one, objects disappear into it. They vanish in an impossible manner, at an increasingly perplexing rate.

You need about forty raisins.

Step 1

- Say, *"The secrets of the Bermuda Triangle are easy to demonstrate. People don't realize that the triangle itself is one of the most traveled areas of the sea. It's no wonder that boats and planes are missing; so many boats and planes go through it."*

- As you are saying this, lay out the triangle with the raisins. This can be done on a table, with a triangle about 18 inches on each side.

Step 2

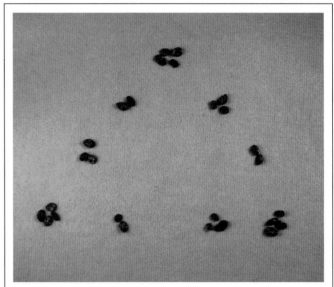

- Each leg of the triangle consists of four distinct piles of raisins. In the corner is a pile of four raisins, then next to it a pile of three, a pile of two, and another pile of four in the next corner.

- When the triangle is constructed, you'll have a total of nine piles. Forming the three points of the triangle are three piles of four raisins each. Between each of them are two piles of two and three.

180

Vonetta was not just a magician but also a "protean artist." In her act she instantly changed costumes to assume different roles. She started her career as a dancer and singer. These skills gave her good experience for music hall performances. When she later added magic to her repertoire, one of her specialties was called The Flags of All Nations, in which she produced hundreds of silk flags that seemed to fill the entire stage. Vonetta accompanied her act with amazing costume changes; it was said that she made twenty-four different changes of costume within the space of a few minutes.

Step 3

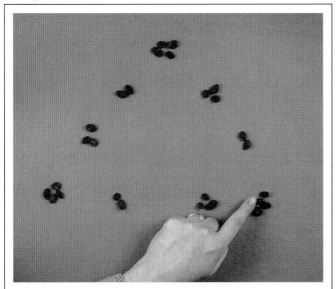

- Point out how the triangle is constructed of three rows of thirteen and count each row, starting at a corner, saying, *"1, 2, 3, 4 . . . 5, 6 . . . 7, 8, 9 . . . 10, 11, 12, 13."*

Step 4

- Hand another raisin (from the extras in your hand) to a spectator. Ask him to place it onto any pile. He does.

- Based on his selection, you make several moves, shifting raisins from one pile to another. When you recount the rows, the just-added raisin seems to have disappeared. In each direction, the rows still contain thirteen raisins. The basic secret consists of shifting raisins away from the corners (where they count twice) to one of the two piles comprising the center of each row (where they count once).

IN THE BERMUDA TRIANGLE (continued)

Some years ago I published a book entitled *Life Savers,* written by an ingenious magician and attorney from California, Michael Weber. In it, he details a way of doing this routine in reverse, starting with the maximum amount of raisins already on the table—it was his idea to use raisins—and then removing them one at a time while the rows still seemingly contain the same total number of objects. He calls his version To Feed

Many, because you eat the raisins (or offer them to members of the audience) as you remove them from the triangle. (M&Ms will also be welcome!) If you have enough room on the table, you might use Hershey's Kisses rather than raisins or M&Ms—they are more likely to be received with pleasure because they're wrapped.

Step 5

- If the spectator places the raisin on a center pile of two or three, the essential move consists of sliding one raisin from a corner of that row down into the center of an adjoining row. This change can be camouflaged by several other ineffective moves consisting of sliding raisins from a center pile to the other center pile in the same row.

- At the conclusion of these moves, each row will still have thirteen raisins.

Step 6

Two moves are required to keep thirteen raisins in each row here.

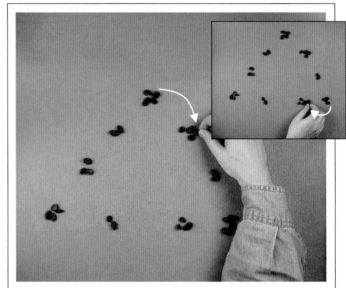

- If the spectator places the object on a corner pile, there are two essential moves in order to make it "disappear." First, move a raisin from that pile down into a center pile (in essence, shifting the spectator's move to a center pile), then move a raisin off that row, from a corner, to a center pile of the adjoining row.

ZOOM

Most of the tricks in this book are a straightforward series of steps. This one, however, requires you to react according to how the spectator places the raisins. Make sure you thoroughly familiarize yourself with the principle used here so you can move the raisins quickly to counteract his additions.

Exactly the same procedure is followed here as before—you must "correct" any move made by the spectator.

Step 7

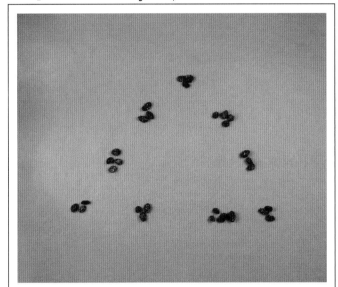

- You will find that the trick can easily be repeated five or six times without seriously affecting the supply of raisins in the corner piles. This is enough to stress the futility of the exercise. The presentation has a great deal to do with it. By quickly counting through the piles, then handing another raisin to the spectator, urging him to do it again, the impossibility of the exercise increases.

Step 8

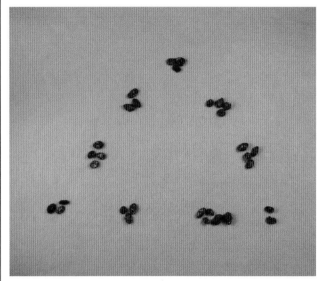

- The spectators will stop you to count the raisins themselves and contemplate the triangle, just as you are urging them to drop another raisin into the mysterious triangle.

- It becomes funnier and stranger as it goes on; after five or six raisins most audiences are convinced that the objects could keep vanishing all evening.

BANANA MYSTERY

Bananas are inherently funny; using them gives you a head start with a presentation

The trick Impromptu Mind Reading described in chapter 10 introduced you to Roy Baker's clever method of forcing a particular object: the PATEO Force—PATEO being an acronym for Pick Any Two Eliminate One.

The idea of having a spectator pick a number, then peeling open a banana to discover that it has been presliced (while sealed in its skin!) into the same number of pieces is an old one. The original involved some skill with sewing; however, wiser heads have since prevailed, and now all you need is a needle (sans thread) to prepare the banana. Combining it

Step 1

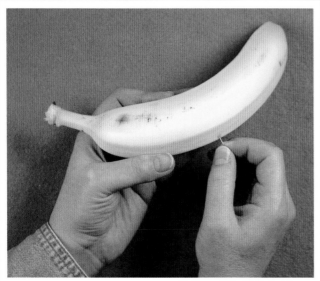

- Use one of your "practice" bananas. You are going to secretly, and in advance, cut it into four pieces while it's still inside the skin. This is done by inserting a sewing needle through one of the ridges until it goes almost all the way through the meat in the center.

- Then waggle the needle neatly from side to side.

- Withdraw it a little and waggle it from side to side again—you get the idea. You must completely sever the banana at that point.

Step 2

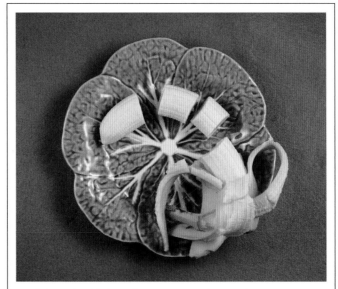

- Afterward, withdraw the needle. Do exactly the same thing two more times at different points along the length of the banana. Because you're just practicing at this point, peel the banana afterward and see if you've been successful: You should have four neatly sliced pieces. With that

understood, prepare one of the four bananas in your attached bunch that way and remember which one it is (you can mark it with your fingernail if that will help you to remember).

with Roy Baker's force makes a neat, simple, and, most important, convincing trick.

You need a bunch of four bananas, a few loose bananas for practice, an opaque handkerchief or cloth that will completely cover them, a sewing needle, a deck of playing cards, and a pencil or indelible marker.

Use red ink to make a mark in the angel's belly button (we've used black in the photo so you can see it clearly).

Step 3

- Spread through your deck of cards and remove the four fours (spades, hearts, clubs, diamonds). Using your pencil or marker, make a tiny dot on the back in an inconspicuous place. The mark must be extremely small. If anyone else sees it but you, your credibility will instantly vanish.

- Once they are marked, place the fours back into the deck and shuffle the cards. You are ready to begin the performance.

Step 4

- Place the bunch of four bananas, covered by the cloth, onto the table. This will immediately create interest and mystery (something under a cloth always does). Bring out the deck of cards and spread it face up between your hands. Say, *"Please select any ace, any two, any three, any four, and any five. It doesn't matter what the suits are, as long as we have one card of each value."*

- Because you have marked the backs of all four fours, it doesn't matter which one of them is chosen.

BANANA MYSTERY (continued)

Using the PATEO technique to force the spectator to select the number four in this particular trick is an easy choice for you because you've learned it in an earlier chapter. Here's a quick refresher on the PATEO Force: You go first—cover two cards but never cover the marked card. The spectator tells you which one to eliminate. Then the spectator covers any two cards. If she covers the marked card, tell her to eliminate the card under her other hand. Repeat this, going back and forth, until only one card remains: the marked card.

Step 5

- Place the deck aside and spread the five cards that have been removed face down on the table. Say, *"I'm going to turn my back, and I want you to mix the cards around as much as you like so none of us have any idea which card is where."*

- Once that's done, face forward and look down—you will immediately see, by locating the mark, which card is the four.

Step 6

Even though you can see the face of the chosen card in the photograph, you wouldn't in real performance.

- Now perform the PATEO Force as explained in chapter 10 in Impromptu Mind Reading. For a quick refresher, look at the top of this page. You never cover the four. If the spectator covers the four, always tell her to remove the other card. This will result in one card remaining on the table—ask the spectator to look at it without showing its face to you. She'll look at the four.

Howard Thurston was America's leading magician through the 1920s. His stage show toured America with dozens of large, colorful illusions, a line of dancers, dozens of costumes, and elaborate scenery. Out of a Hat was a later feature in his show, and this colorful poster gives an impression of the spectacular effect. A gigantic top hat was shown empty. Thurston reached inside to produce parasols and top hats and then flags, silk scarves, and robes. The illusion reached a climax when Thurston discovered three ladies inside the top hat. Yes, indeed: Three ladies came out of the hat!

Step 7

- Say, *"Please remove the cloth from the object on the table."* Once the bananas are revealed, say, *"How many are there?"* If the spectator hasn't already figured out the relationship, say, *"Yes, you chose a four, and there are four bananas. Interesting."*

- Pick up the bunch of bananas and, one at a time, tear off the three that are not prepared and hand them to other audience members. Give the last banana to the spectator who chose the four.

Step 8

- Ask, *"Are you feeling 'fourish'? Not foolish, but fourish—you seem to have an affinity for the number four. The first three people I gave the bananas to, please peel them."*

- Those three bananas will be whole. Turn to the spectator who chose the four and ask her to peel her banana— she will discover that it is in four pieces.

CARD IN ORANGE

This classic is still one of the most impressive tricks in any repertoire

A spectator selects a card, which you then place into a small pay envelope and leave protruding from your pocket. A bowl with some oranges is introduced; the spectator selects one. You make a magical gesture between the pay envelope and the orange. When the spectator tears open the envelope he

finds orange seeds, but no card. You cut open the orange and the chosen card is found inside.

This trick is a wonderful hundred-year-old classic. Finding something inside a naturally sealed object such as a piece of fruit or an egg adds an extra psychological air of mystery,

Step 1

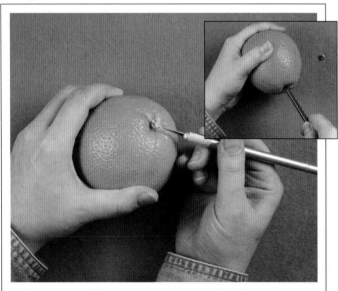

- Prepare one of the oranges by finding the hard nub where it was originally attached to the tree. Using the tip of a knife, carefully pry this nub off the orange without breaking it.

- Once done, shove a thin stick, such as the end of a chopstick or a piece of wire cut from a hanger, straight down into the orange, creating a channel.

Step 2

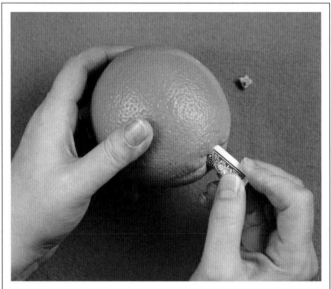

- From one of your decks of cards, remove any card—let's say, as an example, it's the king of clubs. Roll the card, back outward, into as thin a tube as possible and shove it completely inside the channel you've created in the orange. Use a permanent glue to reattach the

nub. Put the loaded orange into the bowl with the other two and make sure you know which one it is—put a small dot on the side with an indelible marker for insurance.

because everyone knows that if you make a hole in an orange or egg, the insides leak out!

You need two small pay or coin envelopes (just large enough for a playing card to slide inside), some seeds that you've removed from an orange in advance and dried, two identical decks of cards, a knife, and a bowl with three oranges.

Step 3

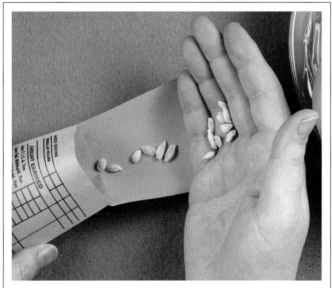

- Prepare one of the envelopes by dropping the dried orange seeds inside. Lick the envelope to seal it and place it in the upper breast pocket of your shirt or jacket (it should be in the pocket of the outermost garment).

Step 4

Here is where the performance of the trick actually begins.

- Begin with the bowl of oranges, the full deck of cards, a knife, and the other envelope. Openly spread through the deck with the faces toward you and locate the king of clubs. Assuming you're going to do the Hindu Shuffle Force explained in chapter 3, simply cut the deck so the king goes to the face. The audience has no idea what you're doing yet, so this action will seem unimportant.

- Now execute the Hindu Shuffle Force so the spectator "selects" the king of clubs, which is removed and placed on the table.

189

CARD IN ORANGE (continued)

Most versions of this trick have you destroy or burn the chosen card—this handling adds an additional magical effect instead. Magic tricks are made more theatrically rich when smaller effects are added within the larger plot. Normally, you might be told to burn the chosen card or make it vanish in some way. Neither is easy—cards don't burn well (the authors who suggest this obviously have never tried it).

Making a card disappear usually requires a piece of magical apparatus that you have to buy (and I'm sure you don't happen to have one in your closet). Jim Steinmeyer suggested the idea of having the chosen card placed into an envelope and changing places with the seeds from the orange. A perfect solution to a vexing problem.

Step 5

Step 6

Make your dot on the loaded orange less obvious than this one!

- Give the chosen king of clubs to the spectator and ask him to insert it into the envelope, then seal it.

- Take the envelope with your right hand and slip it completely into the pocket where the duplicate envelope containing the seeds resides—but you apparently don't let go of it and change your mind. Grasp the "seed" envelope instead and pull it back into view, leaving it sticking out of your pocket, cocked to the side so it doesn't fall back in.

- Gesture toward the bowl of oranges as you begin magician's choice so you end up with the loaded orange. Ask the spectator to *"Grab any two oranges."* If he picks up the two normal fruits, say, *"Please place those aside"* as you pick up the piece of loaded fruit from the bowl. He has no idea what you're going to do, so this seems perfectly natural. Say, *"Grab . . .,"* not *"Choose"* or *"Select."*

- If he picks up the loaded fruit and one normal fruit, say, *"Please place one on the table."* If he places the loaded fruit onto the table, respond, *"Please put the other one back in the bowl."*

Step 7

No matter what happens, you always end up with the loaded orange.

- If he puts the normal fruit onto the table, you pick up the one from the table and put it back into the bowl, saying, *"Hand me the one you've chosen."*

- Make a magical gesture between the orange and the envelope in your pocket.

- Hand the envelope to the spectator and ask him to tear it open and remove the contents. He'll be shocked to discover seeds from the orange.

Step 8

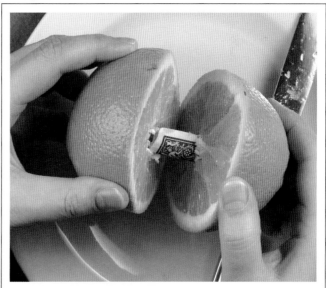

- Wait a few moments and look from him to the orange and back again. If he doesn't take the hint, look from him to the orange again—this will get a chuckle. Take a knife and carefully cut the orange in half, not straight through the center (you don't want to cut the card!), but around the circumference and almost to the center.

- Place the knife aside and use both hands to pull the halves apart to reveal the rolled card inside. Remove the card and unroll it to reveal the chosen king of clubs.

MASTER COIN PENETRATION

A coin penetrates a piece of rubber stretched over a drinking glass

(Created by Lubor Fiedler)

This is the only trick in this book that requires you to purchase something unusual in order to perform it, but it's something dentists use every day that is easily available on the Internet (or from your friendly dentist): dental dam. The illusion that this piece of rubber allows you to perform is one of the most amazing in magic—and happily also one of the simplest.

Step 1

- You need a piece of dental dam 6 inches square. The technical name is "dental dam 6 x 6 medium dark," and it's gray or beige in color.

Step 2

- You also need a quarter, a penny, a drinking glass, and a rubber band.

WHO INVENTED THIS?

European magician and inventor Lubor Fiedler has been dazzling magicians around the world with his ingenuity for decades. He has invented many tricks, and some of the most amazing have been marketed by the Tenyo Company of Japan (available in magic shops and magic Internet sites in the United States). His Blue Crystal, Floating Rock, and Invisible Pen have methods that are as surprising to magicians as the tricks are to the audiences who see them. This particular trick using dental dam is one of his earliest inventions and still among the most clever.

Step 3

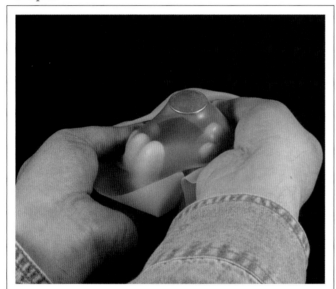

- The most difficult part of this trick is getting set up. Pick up a quarter and balance it on the tip of your right second finger. Grasp the piece of dental dam between the thumbs and fingers of both hands. Stretch the center apart as much as you can until the dam is almost clear and force the quarter up against it from beneath. You'll probably break the first piece you try—either that, or you won't stretch it far enough. You'll have to experiment to figure out just how far you have to stretch the rubber and how hard you have to push up the quarter.

Step 4

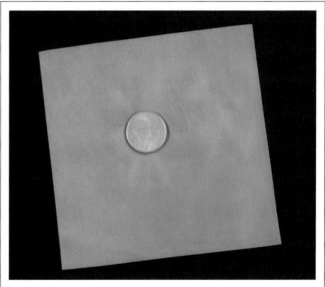

- Allow the dental dam to contract under the quarter. Amazingly, it appears that the quarter is on top of the dental dam rather than under it.

- When this is done properly, the portion of the stretched dental dam that's on top of the quarter is almost invisible.

MASTER COIN PENETRATION (continued)

Dental dam isn't made to be used more than once. Dentists throw it away after each use. As a magician, you'll get more use out of it than that; however, you do have to be careful

because it can break. Fortunately you'll find this out when you're setting up the trick in private rather than when you're in the middle of performing it. So, when you load the quarter into the dam, do so in a slightly different place each time, moving the stress on the rubber to different spots. And don't use the same piece for more than four performances, or else you'll be pressing your luck.

With practice you will actually be able to do this part of the set-up in front of the audience, making it look as if you're holding the quarter in place on top of the dam as you anchor everything atop the glass with the rubber band.

Step 5

- Place the dental dam on top of the glass so the quarter is centered.
- Place the rubber band around the edge of the glass to hold it in place.

Step 6

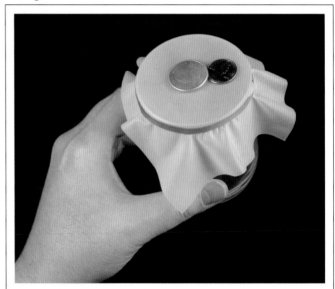

- Place the penny beside the quarter, with its edge just under the larger coin.
- Everything is now set up for the trick.

You can also do this without the glass. Have two spectators each hold two corners of the dental dam so it's flat, but without stretching it. Guide how high or low their hands are held. With the dam held level, you can simply push the quarter through with one finger—or let the spectator push it through.

Step 7

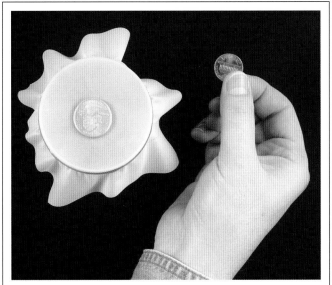

- When it's time to perform this, bring the glass into view and say, *"Please name either the quarter or the penny."* If the penny is named, simply pick it up and hand it to the spectator. If the quarter is named, pick up the penny and just place it aside as you say,

"Then let's use the quarter." This is, again, magician's choice—it doesn't matter which coin the spectator names; the goal is to get the penny out of the way. But it gives the impression that you're giving the spectator a choice.

Step 8

Push the quarter through very slowly! It will appear to melt through the rubber.

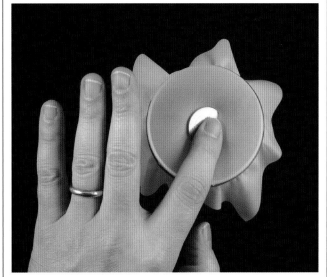

- Put the tip of your first finger onto the center of the quarter and begin to push downward. Do it slowly, pushing until the quarter suddenly disappears—it looks like it melts through the rubber and drops into the glass.

- Immediately hand the glass to the spectator so he can see and hear that the quarter is indeed inside the glass. The rubber band can be removed and the sheet of rubber examined—no hole will be found.

CUPS & BALLS

It's literally, perhaps, the oldest trick in the book but still the most popular

(Created by Richard Kaufman)

In 1983 I developed a new version of the magician's oldest trick, the Cups and Balls, for an expensive Harry Blackstone Jr. magic set manufactured by Pressman Toys for which I wrote the instructions and devised new handlings of many tricks.

While keeping the simplest form of the trick (requiring no

sleight of hand), where the three balls gather and penetrate through three cups, I added a sequence that virtually every professional magician uses to end his or her more complex

Step 1

- You need a set of three cups (paper cups that nest—or stack—work well), four small soft balls of any sort (these can be found at hobby shops), and three pieces of fruit. Each piece of fruit must be small enough to fit inside one of the cups but as large as possible within that restriction.

Small lemons, limes, apples, or potatoes are good.

- You must be seated at a table opposite the audience. Place the three pieces of fruit in your lap.

Step 2

The photo shows just the locations of the balls. The cups are actually stacked and mouth up on the table right now.

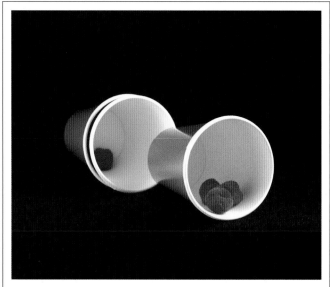

- Stack the three cups, mouth upward. Then drop one of the balls into the center cup and the three remaining balls into the uppermost cup.

routine, where a piece of fruit is magically produced from each cup at the end.

I have updated it slightly for you and am pleased to explain it here. It's not difficult to do by any means; however, the instructions are somewhat lengthy, and it will take practice to learn and perfect the routine. It's best to always think of things like this as a play: Everything must be learned step by step and rehearsed until it is perfected.

Step 3

- Begin by holding the stack of cups in your left hand, mouth upward. Turn the stack over, letting the three balls roll onto the table. The cups are held together so the fourth ball remains securely inside the center cup.

- Turn your left hand back to its original position so the cups are mouth up.

This opening part of the routine should be dispensed with quickly: dump the balls out, show the cups, and put them on the table— all in a nice steady rhythm.

Step 4

- Your right hand takes the bottom cup off the stack and holds it beside the two cups remaining in your left hand.

- Tilt the insides of the cups toward the audience and tap them together. Even though the spectators have seen only the interiors of two cups, they will have the impression that all three are empty. Turn your right hand over and table its cup, mouth downward, on the left.

197

CUPS & BALLS (continued)

You'll learn how to load the first lemon on this page. This takes more courage than most of the things you've learned in this book up to this point; however, you have good misdirective cover by revealing the smaller balls under the cups, and all attention will be on them as you shove the lemon into the cup. Even so, this will take much practice in private before you are ready to perform it for the public.

Step 5

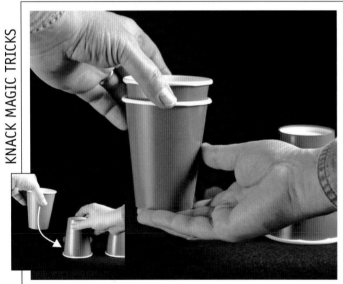

Step 6

Don't tilt the center cup like this. We're doing it only to show you that there's a ball hidden under it.

- Tilt your left hand toward you so the inside of the upper cup is no longer visible to the audience. Turn your right hand palm up and grasp the lowermost cup. Your right hand descends with that cup and smoothly turns palm down, placing the cup on

- the table to the left of the first cup.

- When this is done without pausing, gravity will keep the hidden ball inside the cup.

- Your left hand once again tilts the interior of the cup it still holds toward the audience, then turns the cup mouth downward and tables it to the left of the other two.

- The center cup has the fourth ball secretly concealed beneath it.

198

Everything you've learned before in this book has prepared you for this moment: The full attention of the spectators must be focused on the red ball as it's revealed under the cup in order to provide misdirection for the loading of the lemon.

Step 7

Direct all of your attention to your right hand as it lifts the cups to reveal a ball. Pretend your left hand doesn't even exist.

Step 8

- Pick up one of the three balls from the table and place it on top of the center cup. Your left and right hands grasp the two side cups and stack them on top of the center cup.

- Lower your left hand into your lap. Because your left hand was involved in a downward movement to stack a cup on the center cup, it just continues naturally downward; the rising right hand will catch the eye of the audience.

- Say, *"The first ball will penetrate through the bottom cup."* At the same time, your left hand picks up the first piece of fruit and moves upward until it is just beneath the table edge.

- Snap your right fingers, then lift the stack of upside-down cups with your right

hand. As they're raised, use the inner edge of the lowermost cup to knock the ball beneath it forward. It'll roll a bit, and, under this misdirection your right hand moves to the table edge, and then below it just a bit, where your left hand loads the first piece of fruit into the bottom cup.

199

CUPS & BALLS (continued)

Loading the second lemon is much like the first. The timing and misdirection are the same and still equally effective. Never look down at the hand loading the fruit into the cup! Always watch the ball on the table and the audience.

Step 9

- Your right hand immediately tilts the upper end of the stack of cups (their bottoms) toward the audience. Say, *"Perhaps I fooled you because I used three cups. I'll place one of these cups aside and use only two."*

- Your left hand slides the loaded cup out from inside the stack as you move your left pinky around the edge.

Step 10

Even though the cup with the fruit inside is now much heavier than before, it must not look heavier to the audience.

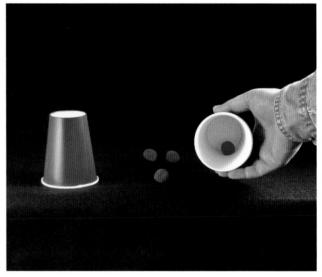

- Your left hand turns to place the cup mouth downward on the table off to the left—your pinky prevents the fruit from falling out prematurely. Also, your right hand must keep the cups it holds tilted far enough forward (mouths toward you) so that the ball

concealed in the cup closest to you doesn't roll out.

- Your left hand now returns and grasps the outermost (empty) cup. Separate the cups, keeping the open ends toward you, and tap them together.

Hieronymus Bosch's late-fifteenth-century image of a conjurer shows him performing Cups and Balls for an astonished crowd. Three small balls appear or disappear beneath three metal cups. It might be the oldest trick in magic, with accounts of it from ancient Greece. For centuries, the Cups and Balls was a standard trick at fairgrounds, its purpose being to attract a crowd. Still performed today, the Cups and Balls is considered the test of a skillful magician. Bosch's painting associates the street magician with common criminals—an unfortunate fact of the time. As the crowd watches in amazement, a pickpocket (literally, a "cutpurse") takes advantage of the situation.

Let your left hand drop straight down into your lap as if it's dead weight after it has stacked the cup.

Step 11

- Your right hand turns its cup mouth down and tables it over the single ball.

- Because there is a ball concealed inside it, there are now two balls beneath the cup. Your right hand immediately picks up one of the two other small balls

that are off to the side and places it on top of the cup.

- Your left hand turns its cup mouth downward and drops it over the cup with the ball sitting on top. Without pausing, your left hand continues downward into your lap and picks up the second piece of fruit.

Step 12

- Simultaneously raise your right hand, snap your fingers, and announce that the second ball will penetrate the cup. Your right hand lifts both cups and knocks the two balls beneath them forward.

- All eyes will be on them as they roll and your right hand moves back to the table edge, and a bit below it, where your left hand loads the second piece of fruit into the lowermost cup.

CUPS & BALLS (continued)

Two lemons are loaded and only one to go! You probably feel like you're trekking through the desert in a long trick like this, where you have certain easy actions to follow that lead up to something "big" that must be done, and then the process starts over again. That's why even though the process of making the small balls penetrate the cups is essentially self-working, this is a difficult routine because it's long—you have to remember all the steps and execute them in order. And

then you have to load the lemons into the cups throughout the routine in order to set up the climax. And you have to make it look effortless—there can be no forgetting, no fumbling, no sense of guilt on your part for the audience to perceive. Perform this routine to perfection, and you can truly call yourself an accomplished magician.

Step 13

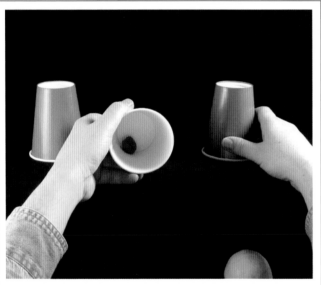

- Say, *"Still a mystery? Let's eliminate a second cup—now there's only one!"* Your right hand tilts both cups forward so the mouth of the lower cup is toward you.

- Your left hand grasps both cups so your right hand can withdraw the cup containing the fruit and table it to the right (keep your pinky beneath to hold the fruit inside). Naturally, your left hand must keep the remaining cup tilted forward so the concealed ball doesn't drop out.

Step 14

We've tilted the cups forward in the photo so you can see where everything is—normally at this point they'd be flat on the table.

- Your left hand now turns its cup mouth downward and lowers it over the two balls (which have already penetrated) on the table.

- At this point the cups on the extreme right and left each contain a piece of fruit. The center cup contains three small balls. The fourth small ball is visible on the table, and the third piece of fruit is on your lap.

- Pick up the last small ball and place it on top of the center cup. Say, *"It's going to be tough to make this last ball go through with only one cup.*

Many of Chung Ling Soo's illusions were elegant and artistic, reminding his audiences of exotic Oriental culture. One of his specialties was a version of the bullet-catching feat. Two marked bullets were loaded into rifles. Chung Ling Soo took his place on the opposite side of the stage, holding a porcelain plate. The gunmen aimed at the plate and fired. Soo caught the bullets on the plate and offered them for examination. One night in London in 1918, he was fatally shot onstage while performing this effect. Although he had planned the trick meticulously, that night his special gun misfired, and he was killed.

Step 15

- *"Hmm . . . You don't mind if I cheat, do you? I'll just stick it under like this."*

- Take the ball off the cup and openly slip it beneath, being careful not to expose the other balls.

- Relax your left hand and let it drop into your lap as you lean forward to ask the spectators, in a whisper, *"How many balls do you think are under the center cup now?"*

- At the same time your left hand picks up the final piece of fruit. Your right hand lifts the center cup to reveal four balls—a surprise to the audience.

Step 16

- Your right hand moves back to the table edge, and a bit below it, so your left hand can load the final piece of fruit beneath the cup. Your right hand replaces the cup on the table just behind the four small balls.

- Finally, mention that you never go anywhere without your lunch and lift the three cups to reveal the fruit.

RUBBER PENCIL

One of the oldest optical illusions still makes a fine magical effect

This is, literally, the simplest trick in the world. It is perfect for the young magician who wants to be able to perform a trick almost immediately after learning it. However, like any trick, it must be done in exactly a certain way to create the proper illusion. Closely following the instructions here will create success and encourage your junior magician to take on more challenging effects.

Step 1

- This amazing optical illusion can be performed with any hard, straight object that is 6 to 12 inches long.

- You can use a spoon, a pen, pencil, a chopstick, or a magic wand.

Step 2

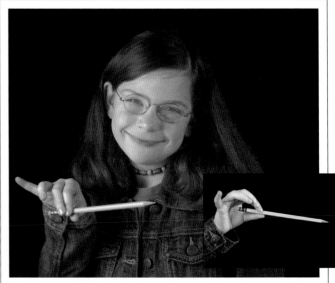

- Let's assume you're going to use a pencil—they're easy to find around the house.

- Begin by lightly gripping the pencil between your right first finger and thumb about 1 inch to the left of the eraser. Your palm is held directly toward the spectators so they see exactly what you see in this photograph.

Sometimes it's hard for a kid to understand that the pencil has to be held very loosely so it can waggle up and down. Be patient in your teaching—learn the trick first yourself and then teach the child.

Keep the pencil horizontal with the spectators' eye line.

Step 3

- This is what it looks like from your point of view.

Step 4

- Begin rapidly jiggling your hand up and down about an inch in each direction. In other words, go up 1 inch, then down 1 inch.

- Do this quickly while holding the pencil loosely. The ends of the pencil will see-saw up and down, and it will appear that the pencil is bending as if it's made of rubber.

KIDS PERFORM MAGIC

205

THE CANNIBAL'S FINGER
Disembodied digits definitely delight

I've been carrying around a box with my finger in it since I was eight years old. Really! When I was very young my parents eventually tired of my pleading and relented by purchasing the Scholastic book *Spooky Magic*. Ever since then I've often carried a little box in my pocket just for this trick because kids love it. They're curious, they laugh, some scream . . . what more could you want? What happens? The young magician holds out a small closed box for display. She lifts the lid and inside, lying on a bed of cotton, is (she says) the finger of an ancient cannibal. The audience sees a gray and dusty-looking disembodied finger—which moves slightly, causing the audience to jump in horror. Taking advantage of the chaos, the magician appears to eat the disembodied finger.

Step 1

- You need a small cardboard box with a removable lid of the type in which earrings are often sold—it should measure about 2½ by 3 inches and be about 1 inch deep. There's usually a layer of cotton inside.
- (If your young magician has a small hand, then use a smaller box.)

Step 2

- Cut a hole in the bottom of the box and the cotton that's the tiniest bit larger than the diameter of the child's second (middle) finger.

You can use your imagination here and apply as much or as little makeup to the finger as you want. If you want to make it a green monster finger, please feel free!

Step 3

The ickier the finger looks, the more effective the trick will be.

Step 4

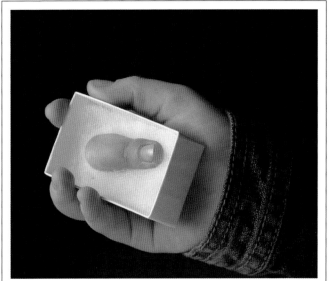

- Using watercolor or tempera, paint the child's second finger a light shade of gray from the center knuckle all the way down to the tip.

- You can also add a little red paint to the cuticle if you're feeling playful. You also need a stick of gum—most gum is grayish in color, perfect for this.

- Insert the child's painted finger up through the hole in the bottom of the box, through the cotton.

- Curl the finger flatly against the cotton so it looks like it's lying in the box. The thumb and other fingers hold the box in place.

THE CANNIBAL'S FINGER (continued)

To this standard trick, which amuses kids, I've added a piece of gum to bring it up to date and give it that extra ghoulish touch that things now require. You don't have to hide the gum: Because it's gray, it looks kind of like your painted finger, and it isn't seen long enough to be recognized. It looks like you lift the finger and pop it into your mouth. When you do this, tilt your right palm slightly toward you so the inside of the box is no longer visible. Then allow your right hand to drop to your side so the underside of the box isn't seen.

Step 5

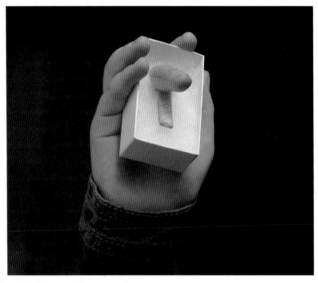

- The last touch is to tuck the stick of gum under the finger, between it and the cotton. It's important to trim the gum if necessary so it doesn't protrude from beneath the finger and can't be seen.

- Place the lid onto the box.

Step 6

- The child brings the box out of her pocket and holds her right hand palm up in front of her. She removes the lid with her left hand to display the finger inside and says, *"On a recent trip to the Amazon jungle, I was able to purchase a cannibal's finger."* Put the lid down.

Step 7

Our little cannibal is showing how you lift the gum out from under the finger, but you really want to tilt the inside of the box toward you.

Step 8

Note how our little cannibal holds the box so the audience can't see either under it or inside.

- She lets the people look at it for a moment, then twitches the finger slightly.

- She inserts her left thumb and first finger into the box as if to grab the finger—but actually grabs only the gum beneath.

- She quickly lifts the piece of gum straight up (she'll have to uncurl her right second finger for a second in order to do this) and pops it into her mouth as she says, *"Whoever owns the cannibal's finger becomes a cannibal, too!"*

- To conclude, she puts the lid onto the box and sticks it into her pocket.

CRYING GEORGE

Making a quarter "cry" is a great beginner's trick

This is a lovely trick for the young magician: The image of George Washington on a quarter seems to cry real tears when you squeeze it. It works as a magical effect because it's unexpected—it never occurs to anyone in advance that real water is going to drip from a coin. And it lets a young magician do a trick with an ordinary object that everyone has in his or her pocket. It's not only for kids—any adult can use this as a humorous gag. If you're sitting in a restaurant, you can

do this off the cuff by tearing off the corner of a paper napkin while it's in your lap and surreptitiously dampening it. Then borrow a quarter and let it "cry." It's easy to let the little wet piece of napkin fall in your lap afterward.

You need a small piece of cotton that you have soaked in water. Place it inside a small "snack"-size Ziploc bag.

Place the Ziploc bag into your lap or right trousers or jacket pocket.

Step 1

- Just before you want to perform this trick, put your right hand into the Ziploc bag and retrieve the wet cotton.

- Let it rest on the tips of your first and second fingers.

Step 2

This photo is a side view so you can see how the cotton is hidden behind the quarter.

- Say, *"Can I please borrow a quarter?"* When someone offers you a quarter, take it with your left hand. Lay the quarter on top of the wet cotton in your right hand so the side with George's face is upward. Do not let the cotton be seen before the quarter is over it.

- Face slightly to the right and raise your right hand beside you, so the face of the quarter is directly toward the spectators and the coin is held vertically.

210

THE ART OF MAGIC

English performer Talma, born Mary Ford, was married to Belgian magician Servais Le Roy. She was billed as the Queen of Coins. Although there have been few successful female magicians, Talma proved the exception. Despite having small hands, she was able to perform intricate coin manipulations with ease, matching many of her male counterparts, and became one of the best-known female magicians. She co-starred with her husband and rotund comic magician Leon Bosco. Their billing was "Le Roy, Talma and Bosco" in a touring stage show in which the trio performed not only individually but also together in various specially written vignettes.

Step 3

- Say, *"We all know that George Washington was a great president, but he was melancholy because of all the trouble he faced. Sometimes he even cried."*

- As you reach the end of that sentence, squeeze the cotton against the back of the quarter and water will drip off the bottom of the coin.

Step 4

- Use your right thumb to push the quarter off your fingertips and onto the table—your thumb will automatically cover the piece of cotton as it pushes the quarter.

- Once the quarter is out of your hand, you can let your hands drop to your lap or to your sides and get rid of the cotton.

PHANTOM TUBE

A quick prop with cardboard and glue allows you to do dozens of tricks

There are certain magician's props that can do lots of different things—we call them "utility" items. The Phantom Tube is well over one hundred years old and is sold at magic shops as a large painted metal tube. However, you can fool even someone who owns one if you make a Phantom Tube out of an everyday object—like a cereal box. Kids are always completely fooled because they all know what a cereal box is, and it seems entirely innocent to them. The construction is simple, and, once made, it works by itself—perfect for a young magician.

Step 1

- You need two identical cereal boxes, scissors, and glue stick. Remove the contents of both cereal boxes.

- We'll leave one box as is for the moment, but carefully open the bottom as well as the top.

- From the other box, you're going to cut away everything and leave only the front panel and a small angled portion of each side panel.

Step 2

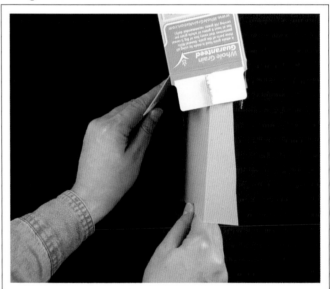

- Turn the cut-out panel gray side up and bend the side panels downward along the natural crease of the box. Apply the glue stick liberally to the gray sides of the side panels.

- Slide the panel inside the whole cereal box at an angle. The gray interior of the panel should face inside the box. The lower end of the inserted panel is pressed firmly against the bottom forward edge of the box.

- Also put some glue on the underside (the printed side) of the outer end of the panel—its narrowest point.

Step 3

Make sure you get the secret panel in position inside the box before the glue has a chance to dry.

- The upper end of the panel is tilted inward so it's about 1 inch away from the front panel of the whole box, creating a compartment. Once the panel is in position, press the outer end against the inside of the front of the box with your thumbs so it adheres firmly in place. Also press the glued side flaps firmly against the side flaps of the whole box. Let it dry, close the flaps on the top and bottom, and your Phantom Tube is ready.

Step 4

The upper photo is what the audience sees—an apparently empty box. The lower photo is what you see—the secret compartment.

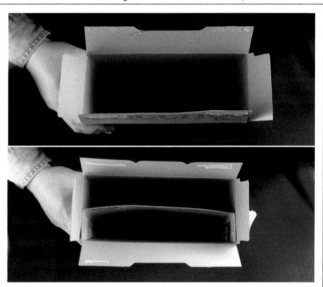

- Here's how the Phantom Tube works. Hold it so the front of the cereal box faces the audience. Open the flaps on top, then open the flaps on bottom.

- Now raise the bottom of the box so it points directly toward the spectators—they will see an empty box. You, on the other hand, will see two compartments.

PHANTOM TUBE (continued)

You don't want the items in the compartment to fall out when you tilt the upper end of the box toward you, so it helps to hold the box higher to enable the spectators to see through it so you do not have to tilt it back a full 90 degrees. It also helps if you don't fill the secret compartment completely full. Also, make sure you keep the box right side up.

On this page are some tricks that you can do with your Phantom Tube. All of them are based on the fact that you can hide things inside the secret compartment while being able to show the box empty to the audience. You can also divide the hidden compartment in two and do additional tricks: Make your prop out of a box for powdered laundry soap. Cut a small piece of cardboard and use it to create a divider down the center of your secret compartment. Have three clean

Step 5

- Magical production of cereal or candy: Before you start, fill the secret compartment with cereal or wrapped candies.

Step 6

- Close the top and bottom before you begin. To perform, open the top and bottom of the box and raise the bottom so the audience can see through it—it's empty.

white hankies in the right side of the secret compartment. Begin by showing the box of soap powder empty. Close the bottom. Insert three white hankies, on which you've previously made all sorts of hideous stains, into the left side of the secret compartment. Snap your fingers, shake the box, then bring the clean hankies out of the right side of the compartment. Open the bottom of the box and show it empty.

Magically Dying Handkerchiefs: Your Phantom Tube has the

small cardboard divider down the center of your secret compartment. Put three small color handkerchiefs in the right side of the compartment in advance. Begin by showing the box empty. Turn it upright and close the bottom. Insert three white hankies into the left side of the secret compartment one at a time. Snap your fingers; then bring out the colored handkerchiefs from the right side of the compartment. Open the bottom and show the box empty afterward.

Step 7

- Rotate it until it's upright, then close the top and bottom. Say your magical word, then open the top of the box.

- Turn the box upside down over a bowl and pour out the treats.

Step 8

- Torn and restored newspaper: Take one page of a newspaper and fold it up so it's small enough to fit into the secret compartment. Begin by showing the box empty, then close the bottom. Take an identical newspaper page and tear it into little pieces, then drop it into the secret compart-

ment. Mysteriously wave your hand over the top of the box, then bring out the whole page and unfold it to reveal the restoration. Show the box empty.

REMOVING YOUR FINGER
Although adults think this is silly, kids are amazed by it

You've seen lots of people do this badly: pretend to pull off a finger or thumb. When done poorly, it's at best a gag and at worst just dumb. However, I've been doing this for many years, and it's one of the most amazing things you can do for kids if you follow the instructions closely and do it well. Why are kids amazed by it? Because you are defying a natural law they inherently understand by the time they're five or six years old: You cannot remove a part of your body and put it back on. It rocks their little world when the tip of your finger comes off. Be prepared for them to ask you to repeat it fifty times—but don't do it!

Step 1

- Hold your right hand in front of you, fingers straight and together.
- Cover it with your left fingers (held the same way but pointing downward) from the front.

Step 2

- Quickly curl your right first finger in half at the center joint.

The goal in this step is to substitute the end of your left thumb for the end of your right first finger. Your left fingers shield this action from the audience, though they have been moved out of the way for this photograph.

Step 3

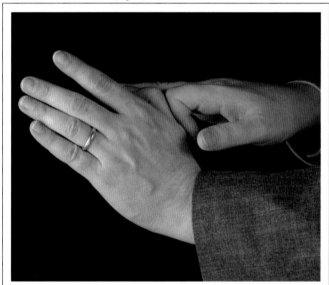

- Bend your left thumb so the tip lies along the upper side of your right second finger, and the thumb presses flatly against the bent portion of the right first finger.

If you really look at this critically, the tip of your thumb doesn't much resemble the tip of your first finger. It doesn't matter!

Step 4

- Lower your left first fingertip over the joint where the knuckles of the left thumb and right first finger meet while opening your other left fingers.

- As you can see from the photo, this looks quite convincing to an audience.

REMOVING YOUR FINGER (continued)

Although adults from Western countries have seen this done umpteen times (and often badly), adults from other parts of the world are often fooled by this simple trick. There is an entire category of magic known as "finger tricks," which is a subset of the even larger category of tricks done with body parts. Many of these can be found in Martin Gardner's book *Encyclopedia of Impromptu Magic*. British TV producer and magic historian John Fisher even wrote an entire book on the subject, aptly entitled *Body Magic*.

Unfortunately both of these books are long out of print; however, if you search the Internet for "magic tricks with your body," you'll find lots of fun illusions to do with your head, fingers, arms, and so on.

Step 5

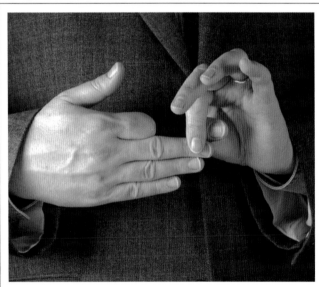

- While keeping your left thumb tip pressed firmly downward on the upper side of your right second finger, slide it to the left.

- The photo shows how effective the illusion is to the audience—it genuinely looks as if your finger has been divided in half.

Step 6

- Don't stay in that position for more than a second or two and be careful not to allow the child to see either the bent tip of your right first finger or the bent length of your left thumb. Seeing either will destroy the illusion instantly.

- Slide your left hand to the right until your left thumb bumps up against your right first finger—where you started a moment ago. Rapidly lower your left fingers in front of your right fingers.

THE ART OF MAGIC

Servais Le Roy was an inventive Belgian magician who created many of the most famous illusions of the early twentieth century. His show was known for its lavish production values and surprising, amazing magic. This poster shows a Le Roy creation. An upright piano, played by Le Roy's wife, Talma, was lifted into the air on a small platform. Curtains surrounded the piano as she continued to play a melody. Suddenly the music stopped, and the curtains fell away, showing that the lady and the piano both had disappeared. Le Roy's poster not only shows the illusion but also portrays the astonished audience.

Step 7

- Immediately uncurl your left thumb to get it out of the way, then straighten your right first finger.

- Both of these actions occur behind your left fingers and are not seen by the children.

Step 8

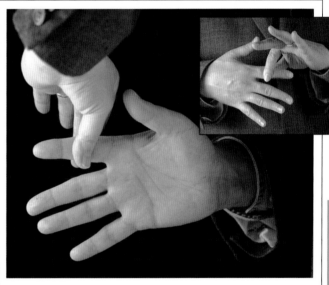

- Your left thumb and first fingertip grasp the center joint of your restored right first finger as you open all your fingers wide.

- The steps shown in the last two photos are really an almost instantaneous switch of your left thumb for the right first fingertip so that you can "get out" of this cleanly and complete the mystery by restoring your finger in a magical way.

THE MAGIC BOOK

Shakespeare probably saw this trick, which is just as good today as it was 400 years ago

In Reginald Scot's 1584 book *Discoverie of Witchcraft,* instructions are clearly given on how to make what is called a "Blow Book." It is a magical book that allows you to flip through the pages and show images that change each time you go through it. Here is a simplified version that not only you but also a child could perform (although you'll have to take care of the preparation). The instructions take you through the essential steps of how to make and use the book—I leave the exact presentation up to you. The more personalized you can make it for a performance, the better. If you're going to perform for a group of young girls, ages four to seven, for example, then making pictures of princesses appear will be popular.

Step 1

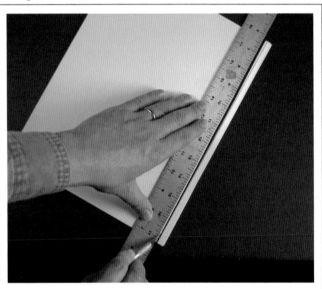

- You need twenty pieces of letter-size (8½ x 11 inch) white paper, two pieces of colored construction paper of the same size, and a heavy-duty stapler (or three brass cotter pins).

- Take ten sheets of the white paper and carefully slice ⅛ inch off one long side using an X-acto knife and a straight edge. If you're an adult, be careful! **If you're a kid, let an adult do it.**

Step 2

- Assemble the book by alternating the ten trimmed pages with the ten untrimmed pages: The first page should be untrimmed, and the second page trimmed. If done properly, the last page will be a trimmed one.

- Place one piece of construction paper at the front and the other at the back of your book.

220

The most famous version of this type of Blow Book, *The Magic Magic Book,* was created by magician Ricky Jay in 1994 and published in the Writers and Artists Series of the Whitney Museum of American Art. Famous modern artists including Vija Celmins, Jane Hammond, Glenn Ligon, Justin Ladda, Philip Taaffe, and William Wegman contributed original artwork to *The Magic Magic Book,* which was published in a limited edition of 300 copies and sold for $1,500 each. In addition to the Blow Book, a separate book written by Mr. Jay described the history of this unique type of magic book and was included in the clamshell box covered in fancy cloth. One of the most beautiful magic books ever published, *The Magic Magic Book* now sells for many times its original price among collectors.

Step 3   Cut the pages neatly and carefully!

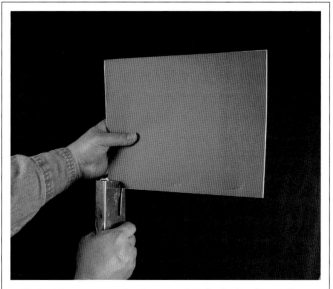

- Gather the pages so they're squared into a neat pile. Now turn them and tap one of the long sides downward against the table.

- Staple the book together at the long side that you've just tapped on the table (and make sure to keep all the pages lined up when you do this). If you're using cotter pins instead of staples, you should use a hole punch prior to inserting the pins.

Step 4

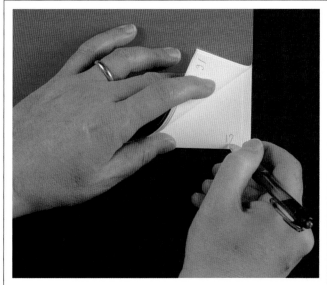

- Let's consider the book you've just made a sample to learn how this works. Place it onto the table in front of you, stapled long side to the left, and open the cover as if it's a normal book. Using a pencil, lightly write small page numbers at the bottom corner of each page, starting with the first white page on your right. The last page, facing the back cover, should be numbered "40."

THE MAGIC BOOK (continued)

Next, just as an example, write an enormous X on pages 2–3, 6–7, 10–11, 14–15, 18–19, 22–23, 26–27, 30–31, 34–35, 38–39. All the other pages are left blank. Of course, when you actually use this book in a performance, you should glue, say, black-and-white pictures to the pages noted earlier and color pictures on the other pages—then the black-and-white pictures will magically turn to color the second time you flip through the book. Or you can leave every other page blank and write the birthday child's name on the pages noted earlier. This is a versatile prop that can accommodate numerous customized presentations, depending upon the occasion.

Step 5

- To show that all the pages in the book have Xs, grasp the stapled long side of the book with your left hand.

- Your right hand grasps the right long side of the book, thumb on the edges of the pages.

Step 6

- Bend the right long side of the book downward and allow the pages to riffle one at a time slowly off your right thumb. Every page in the book will appear to have an X on it. What's actually happening is that each time a page flicks past your right thumb, it's actually two pages—this occurs

because the second page is narrower than the first in each pair.

It will feel funny to flip through the pages with opposite hands the first few times, but it will soon seem perfectly natural.

- To show that all the pages in the book are blank, your hands reverse positions. In other words, your right hand grasps the left stapled edge by reaching around from the back, while your left hand grasps the right long side by reaching around from the front.

Don't flip through the pages so quickly that the audience can't see what's on them!

- Pull upward with your left thumb and allow the pages to flip off it from the back of the book to the front. This time all the pages will appear blank.

- Magic dealers sell these type of books pre-made and rather inexpensively. They are often called "Magic Coloring Books."

MAGIC PRODUCTION TUBES
Kids love this trick because they get candy

Display two empty tubes—packages of Quaker Oats cereal, neither of which has a top or bottom. Showing the interior of each, you pass them through one another to prove they're empty. Nesting one inside the other, you produce handfuls of jelly beans.

You need two empty Quaker Oats tubes of the same size, from which you've removed the tops and bottoms. Now you must make a vertical cut through the back of one of the tubes

and remove a slice about ¼ inch wide. Reattach the sides using packing tape. You've reduced the diameter and created a smaller tube that will slide through the larger tube.

You also need a piece of heavy wire 5 inches long, cut from a metal clothes hanger. Take the 5-inch piece of heavy wire and bend ½ inch of each end in opposite directions.

A Ziploc snack bag and some jelly beans complete the requirements.

Step 1

- Cut the Ziploc bag down in size slightly by slicing off part of the side and bottom. Seal those with packing tape. Now fill it with jelly beans and zip the top closed.

- Paint the insides and upper edges of both tubes as well as the metal rod with the bent ends matte black.

Step 2

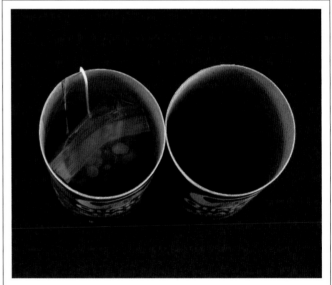

- Poke one end of the metal wire through the Ziploc bag, just below the zipline. (You may need to reinforce the plastic on either side of the hole you're making with some packing tape.)

- Lower the bag into the small tube and hook the other end of the wire over the edge. Place the two tubes side by side on the table.

In all the photographs we've left the inside of the tubes and the metal wire unpainted so you can see what's happening. But remember that these would be black so the wire isn't seen by the audience.

Step 3

You're passing one tube through the other to prove that they're empty.

Step 4

- Pick up the small tube with your right hand, holding it near the top, and the large tube with your left hand, holding it near the bottom.

- Tilt the bottom of the large tube toward the spectators so they can see that it's empty.

- Turn the large tube upright and insert the lower end of the small tube into it. Push the small tube downward.

- When the tubes nest perfectly, the hooked end of the wire will fit over the edges of both tubes.

MAGIC PRODUCTION TUBES (continued)

The great thing about these tubes is that, once you make them, you can use them to produce just about anything that will fit in the Ziploc bag that hangs inside. You could produce oatmeal (if you really wanted to go for an organic presentation) or handkerchiefs (you could squash a lot of thin ladies' silk hankies into the bag) or anything else you can think of. If you want to produce a larger load, then make the tubes yourself out of larger pieces of heavy cardboard (using a larger Ziploc bag as well). It might be easier to make square tubes (boxes, really, without tops or bottoms) rather than round ones if you do it yourself. The tubes can be made large enough to produce a dozen cupcakes, for example, or a large plush toy for the birthday child.

Step 5

- Transfer your grip so that your right hand is now holding the large tube, and your left hand is ready to receive the small tube as it begins to slide out the bottom of the large tube.

- Lower your left hand to let the small tube come out. The end of the wire catches on the large tube, and the Ziploc bag remains inside it while the small tube moves downward.

Step 6

- Once your left hand has a grip on the small tube, pull it completely out the bottom of the large tube and show it empty.

- Place the small tube upright onto the table. Then, using both hands, guide the large tube over the small tube. The Ziploc bag will bump slightly as it descends past the upper edge of the small tube, but that should not disturb it as long as you don't lower the large tube too quickly.

Some loads don't require using the Ziploc bag. If you've tightly bundled up some silk handkerchiefs with rubber bands around them, and slipped one of the rubber bands over the lower hook on the metal wire, now is when you would remove the rubber bands before pulling out the hankies.

Some parents might prefer if you produce wrapped candies for their kids.

Step 7

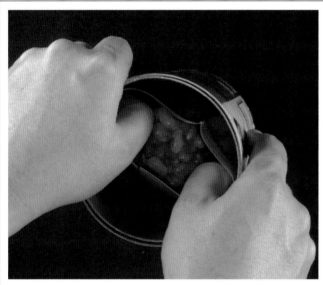

- Once both tubes are nested, make a magic pass over them.

- Reach inside and open the top of the Ziploc bag.

Step 8

- Reach inside and bring out a large handful of jelly beans and let them cascade to the table.

A LAST WORD

And here we are, sixty tricks later.

Some books like to tout the enormous number of tricks they teach—"100!" "200!" But what's the point if the tricks are explained inadequately or if half of them are optical illusions or puzzles and not magic?

I've taken a different approach here, moving you very slowly through each and every step of the process in learning the tricks, the presentation, and the patter required so that you can actually perform them, not just glance at the book or get frustrated due to inadequate instructions and put the book on your shelf.

It's also vital to recognize the importance of the photographs in a work like this. No matter how much I write about something, there will always be additional information captured in the visual images, so study them well.

You may be wondering what the next step is if you've learned one or more of the tricks in this book:

"If I learn two, do I just perform them one after another?"

"Which tricks sort of fit together if I want to make a small show out of it?"

"I really like this and want to buy some stuff!"

"Where are all the other magicians in the world?"

Take heart! We've all asked those questions when starting in magic. Fortunately the answers are easy to come by because this chapter is designed to give you the resources you need.

I'll leave you with two simple statements that have been repeated throughout this book and bear repeating again. They are the most valuable secrets we have:

The most important things about performing magic are personality, presentation, effect, and method—in that order.

And practice makes perfect. But you already knew that.

Richard Kaufman

ROUTINING MAGIC

How important is it to be able to fit your tricks together, like pieces of a puzzle, so you get a proper performance out of them rather than just a hodgepodge? Very important—so important, in fact, that my old and long-deceased friend Señor Mardo (who was not only a magician but also a spy) wrote one of the most highly regarded books about the subject, aptly entitled *Routined Magic*.

Sometimes this is an absolute mystery, even to the best magicians. It requires an understanding of the nature of drama and comedy and how to figure out the "beats" in a trick (just like the "beats" an actor finds in a scene—the high and low points, the drama versus the comedy, and so on). It also requires an understanding of your personality and which tricks you find suit you best—I can't help you with those decisions. Experience will give you the answers.

If you wanted to come across as a card expert, then your show should consist entirely of card tricks. Here is a good selection and the order in which you might present them:
1. Chicago Opener
2. Nine Cards
3. Do As I Do
4. My Uncle Cheated at Cards
5. Quadruple Coincidence (or Card in Orange)

Another way to look at it, however, is to mix it up. For example, if you are going to do several close-up tricks for someone, perhaps it's best not to do five card tricks in a row. It's best to do two card tricks, then a coin trick, and possibly a string trick. A show like this might run:
1. Don't Touch the Cards
2. Master Coin Penetration
3. Mr. Jackson Takes a Powder
4. Cell Phone Divination
5. Matrix

If you wish to present yourself as a "mentalist" rather than a magician, then you can do a number of feats of mentalism without doing any magic at all. This type of show might be:
1. Impromptu Mind Reading
2. Thought Speller
3. Professional Spoon Bending
4. Telekinetic Disintegration
5. Cell Phone Divination
6. Precursor to Destiny

If you want to do a show for a larger group of people, here's a good selection:
1. When Planets Align
2. Cut & Restored Rope
3. Precursor to Destiny
4. Hypnotic Ropes
5. Cell Phone Divination
6. Card in Orange

And if you wanted to perform a show just for kids, these are appropriate choices:
1. Vanishing Rope Knot
2. Hypnotic Ropes
3. Cups & Balls
4. The Magic Book
5. Magic Production Tubes

Whatever group of tricks you string together, always try to find some "flow" between them so you can get the props for the previous trick out of the way while introducing those for the next trick.

And remember that you're not just doing a bunch of tricks—it's a show, with a beginning, middle, and end. Start with a short trick to pique interest and save your biggest and best trick for last.

RESOURCES

Featured dealers

Genii, The Conjurors' Magazine

www.geniimagazine.com

Tel. (301) 656-6234

4200 Wisconsin Ave. NW

Suite 106-384

Washington, DC 20016

Genii is the oldest independent magazine devoted to magic and magicians in the world, published since 1936. A one hundred–page glossy color monthly, it delivers feature articles, teaches new tricks, and has reviews of the latest products. The author of *Knack Magic Tricks* (that's me) is also the editor and publisher. If you like this book, you'll enjoy *Genii*. The Genii Corporation also operates The Genii Forum (www.geniimagazine.com/forum), a free online discussion board dedicated to magic (all are welcome), as well as MagicPedia (www.magicpedia.net), the most extensive free online encyclopedia of magic in the world.

HOTTRIX

www.hottrix.com

Entrepreneur, photographer, producer, and magician/comedian Steve Sheraton was ahead of the curve in creating technology-based magic. The pinnacle of his achievements is his magic applications for mobile devices such as the Apple iPhone and iPod. Using the phone as an interactive magic prop, you can apparently drink beer, milk, or five different flavors of soda; turn your iPod into a popcorn machine, then reach through the screen and remove popped kernels to eat; have your favorite celebrities call you on your iPhone; and perform magic with virtual coins, goldfish, or bugs. All these apps require little skill, come with fun instruction videos, and are unique in the field of magic.

Houdini's Magic Shops

www.houdini.com

Tel. (702) 798-4789

With ten locations, this is the largest chain of magic shops in the United States. Run by well-known magician and Las Vegas gambling expert Geno Munari, Houdini's Magic Shops offer a full range of magic props for both professional and amateur magicians on the website and at all their locations in Las Vegas, Disneyland, and Pier 39 in San Francisco, where you can see magicians demonstrate many tricks. Members of their club are able to receive discounts on products, and they also sell many original products.

Jim Steinmeyer/Hahne Publications

www.jimsteinmeyer.com

Fax (818) 563-1757

Jim Steinmeyer is the creator of many of the greatest illusions in the latter half of the twentieth century. He also devises ridiculously clever tricks (two of which you can find in this book) and is the author of numerous books on both the performance—for close-up, stand-up, and stage—of magic and its history, including several biographies. For simple tricks I'd recommend his two *Impuzzibilities* books and for more challenging material his *Conjuring Anthology*.

Kaufman and Company

www.kaufman.geniimagazine.com

Tel. (301) 652-5800

4200 Wisconsin Ave. NW

Suite 106-292

Washington, DC 20016

One of the largest publishers of books on close-up magic for the amateur and professional for over thirty years, operated by Richard Kaufman (that's me again, the writer of this book). Kaufman and Company sells books on all sorts of magic, featuring the most famous magicians in the world, many of which are written by . . . well . . . me! Kaufman and Company also publishes books on the history of magic and its allied arts (such as balloon twisting and séances).

Nielsen Magic

www.nnmagic.com
Tel. (702) 656-7674
P.O. Box 34300
Las Vegas, NV 89133

Do you think the antique magic posters that are reproduced in this book are beautiful? They were all provided by Norm and Lupe Nielsen, who have one of the most remarkable collections of antique magic posters and lithographs in the world. Happily, they reproduce many of them in stunning clarity and sell copies, including posters of Houdini and other famous magicians of the past. They also sell handmade specialized magic props.

Everything you need to be a magician

Alakazam Magic

www.alakazam-usa.com
Tel. (916) 409-9106
P.O. Box 160
Roseville, CA 95661

An online store founded by magician Peter Nardi featuring its own line of unique tricks in addition to general offerings. The site has extensive video demonstrations of its products.

Al Schneider

www.worldmagiccenter.com
An online store where Al Schneider, the creator of Matrix (taught in this book), sells his new creations and ebooks. If you want to learn coin magic, his writings form an excellent path.

Axtell Expressions, Inc.

www.axtell.com
Tel. (805) 642-7282
Some of the most magical puppetry in the world is created by Steve Axtell, including hands-off, remote-controlled figures.

Ben Harris

www.wowbound.com
An online store devoted to the clever magic of creator and author Ben Harris of Australia.

Cannon's Great Escapes

www.CannonsGreatEscapes.com
Internet site selling all the apparatus required to learn the art of escapes, run by well-known escape artist Mark Cannon.

Card-Shark

www.card-shark.de
Tel. (011) 49-201-848-61-61
Christian Schenck
Schliepersberg 43
D-45257 Essen
Germany

A specialized company that sells faux-antique playing cards of its own design that can add a great deal of interest to magical presentations. It also manufactures tricks to match the designs of its playing cards.

The Cuckoo's Nest

www.thecuckoosnest.com
Tel. (412) 481-4411
1513 East Carson St.
Pittsburgh, PA 15203

The Cuckoo's Nest is a general magic dealer that has an online store and a brick-and-mortar magic shop you can visit.

D'Lite

www.dlite.com

If you've ever seen a magician's thumb light up, then you know the product this company created—it has sold millions of them. In addition it has other unique products available.

Elmwood Magic

www.elmwoodmagic.com
Tel. (800) 764-2372
P.O. Box 387
Lancaster, NY 14086

An online general magic shop that carries a full range of props for magicians, many of which can be seen with online video demonstrations.

Fun Inc.

www.funinc.com
Tel. (877) 438-6462

Fun Inc. is a wholesale company that sells to magic shops and toy stores around the world. They own the rights to Glorpy (a wonderful trick explained in this book).

H & R Magic Books

www.magicbookshop.com
Tel. (281) 540-7229
3839 Liles Lane
Humble, TX 77396

An online store that sells new and used instructional magic books and DVDs.

Hank Lee's Magic Factory

www.magicfact.com
Tel. (781) 391-8749
P.O. Box 789
Medford, MA 02155

An online store that sells a wide range of magical products.

Its warehouse at 102 North Street, Medford, is also open on certain days of the week for shopping.

Hermetic Press, Inc.

www.hermeticpress.com
Tel. (206) 768-1688
1500 SW Trenton St.
Seattle, WA 98106

A notable publisher of fine magic books, run by Stephen Minch, one of the best writers in our field.

High Trick Company

www.Hightrick.com

An online store that sells general magic in addition to many stage illusions.

House of Magic

www.houseofmagic.com
Tel. (415) 987-2218
P.O. Box 470817
San Francisco, CA 94147

An online magic shop featuring original items by owner Mark Burger.

International Magic

www.internationalmagic.com
Tel. (011) 44-20-7405-7324
89 Clerkenwell Rd.
London EC1R 5BX
United Kingdom

This is a general magic shop that has both an online shop and a store you can visit to see magic demonstrated. It has been operated by the MacMillian family for many years and also hosts an annual convention.

JB Magic—Mark Mason

www.jbtvusa.com

Tel. (352) 589-2533

Selling mostly his own creations and marketed tricks, Mark Mason has developed a sterling reputation for producing magic that is amazing to see and easy to do.

Kardwell International

www.kardwell.com

Tel. (800) 233-0828

P.O. Box 33

Mattituck, NY 11952

This company sells gambling supplies, including all sorts of playing cards, and also prints customized decks of playing cards.

Kozmo Magic

www.kozmomagic.com

Tel. (607) 725-5377

A producer of magic DVDs.

L&L Publishing

www.llpub.com

Tel. (530) 525-5700

P.O. Box 100

Tahoma, CA 96142

A producer of magic DVDs featuring some of the world's most famous magicians and a publisher of magic books.

Losander, Inc.

www.losander.com

Tel. (702) 492-3535

9850 S. Maryland Parkway

Suite A5 #190

Las Vegas, NV 89183

Dirk Losander is a professional magician and performer and has invented some remarkable things, all of which you'll find for sale here, including his famous Floating Table.

Magic, Inc.

www.magicinc.net

Tel. (773) 334-2855

5082 N. Lincoln Ave.

Chicago, IL 60625

This is a celebrated general magic shop with a long history that has both an online shop and a store you can visit to see magic demonstrated.

Magic Star Studio

www.joemogar.com

Tel. (856) 358-3684

P.O. Box 76

Deerfield, NJ 08313

A famous trick that is outside the realm of this book is the Color-Changing Pocket Knife. Joe Mogar makes the best knives in magic, which he sells on his website, along with his inventions in magic with thimbles.

Magic Ventures

www.magicventures.com

Tel. (702) 897-1224

3518 W. Post Rd.

Las Vegas, NV 89118

Do you have dreams of being an illusionist and doing a stage show? Bill Smith's Magic Ventures is a company that has built many of the illusions you've seen magicians use on TV.

The Magic Warehouse

www.magicwarehouse.com

Tel. (877) 946-2442

11419 Cronridge Dr.

Suite 10

Owings Mills, MD 21117

Located in a suburb of Baltimore, Maryland, this is a general magic shop that has both an online shop and a store you can visit to see magic demonstrated.

Martin Breese International
www.abracadabra.co.uk
19 Hanover Crescent
Brighton, East Sussex BN2 9SB
Publisher of magic books and high-end magician's props in England.

Martinka & Co.
www.martinka.com
Tel. (201) 444-7546
103 Godwin Ave.
Midland Park, NJ 07432
Magicians have been buying magic tricks for about 150 years, and sooner or later much of it is auctioned on this website. From used tricks to expensive posters and valuable antique magic props, owner Ted Bogusta sells it all.

Merchant of Magic
www.magicshop.co.uk
Tel. (011) 44-2392-25-22-20
39 Brambles
Enterprise Centre
Waterberry Dr.
Waterloo, Hampshire P07 6UE
United Kingdom
A large online magic shop offering an extensive selection of tricks, books, DVDs, online downloads, and more.

Midwest Magic
www.midwestmagic.net
Tel. (847) 455-4288
9706 Franklin Ave.
Franklin Park, IL 60131

Located outside Chicago, this is a general magic shop that has both an online shop and a store you can visit to see magic demonstrated.

The Miracle Factory
www.miraclefactory.net
Tel. (877) 707-4268
1905 S. Harvard Blvd.
Los Angeles, CA 90018
Run by Todd Karr, this company publishes magic books and historical CD-ROMS and markets some of its own magic tricks.

Misdirections Magic Shop
www.misdirections.com
Tel. (415) 566-2180
1236 9th Ave.
San Francisco, CA 94122
This is a general magic shop that has both an online shop and a store you can visit to see magic demonstrated.

T. Myers Magic, Inc.
www.tmyers.com
Tel. (800) 648-6221
6513 Thomas Springs Rd.
Austin, TX 78736
Seller of all the paraphernalia required to make balloon animals and sculptures. Also sells material for juggling, face painting, and gospel magic.

Porper Originals
www.porperoriginals.com
Tel. (818) 341-1849
9142 Jordan Ave.
Chatsworth, CA 91311
Joe Porper is famous for making pool cues, but he also designs and hand makes unique tricks of all kinds famous for their high-precision machining.

Sean Bogunia's Ultimate Magic Productions

www.seanbogunia.com

Tel. (800) 766-8187

4716 Niles-Buchanan Rd.

Buchanan, MI 49107

Magician and yo-yo champion Sean Bogunia sells only his own creations, which range from amazing dancing handkerchiefs to floating light bulbs and much more.

Squash Publishing

www.squashpublishing.com

1719 W. Leland Ave.

Chicago, IL 60640

Squash, run by Gabe Fajuri, publishes magic books for amateur and professional magicians.

Tora Magic Company

www.toramagic.org

Located in Iran, this magic company sells only the unusual apparatus it makes. Sales are worldwide.

Wizard Craft Magic

www.wizardcraft.com

Tel. (845) 790-5109

P.O. Box 1557

Pleasant Valley, NY 12569

An online general magic shop run by magician Craig Dickson.

World Magic Shop

www.worldmagicshop.co.uk

Tel. (011) 44-121-333-6400

Unit 1, Rhea Business Park

Inkerman St.

Birmingham B7 4SH

United Kingdom

An online magic shop that produces much of its own acclaimed products, including DVDs and tricks.

Magic Clubs

General clubs you can join

There are two large magic organizations in the United States: the International Brotherhood of Magicians (I.B.M.) and the Society of American Magicians (S.A.M.). Both require dues to join and have local monthly meetings in many cities in the United States and around the world. Both also publish monthly magazines for their members and have conventions on a yearly basis where magicians gather to watch shows and lectures and enjoy the good fellowship of sharing ideas with like-minded folks. Joining a magic club is a great way to meet other people interested in magic, and their monthly meetings are the social network of magic.

International Brotherhood of Magicians

www.magician.org

Tel. (636) 724-2400

13 Point West Blvd.

St. Charles, MO 63301-4431

Society of American Magicians

www.magicsam.com

Tel. (702) 355-0794

10120 W. Flamingo Rd.

Suite #4-118

Las Vegas, NV 89147

Private magic clubs

The two most famous private magic clubs in the world are The Magic Castle in Hollywood, California, and The Magic Circle in London. Membership to both is actively accepted by those with a genuine interest in magic, and an audition is required as part of membership.

The Magic Castle

www.magiccastle.com
Tel. (323) 851-3313
7001 Franklin Ave.
Hollywood, CA 90028

The premier home of magic in the United States, The Magic Castle has been operated by the Academy of Magical Arts, founded by the Larsen family, since 1963. Sitting in a historically designated building in the Hollywood Hills, this exclusive club has multiple theaters, bars, and a restaurant. Many magic shows are performed every night of the week. Entrance is restricted to members, who can also provide special cards to friends that will allow them to make reservations as a guest. Any member of the I.B.M., S.A.M., or The Magic Circle is also welcome to make reservations. The Magic Castle houses a museum and library, and lectures and classes are given. Reservations and dinner are required for non-members, and there is a strict dress code. Those under age 21 are only allowed in the Castle for Sunday Brunch and certain designated events. However, there is a special club for younger magicians called "Castle Juniors."

The Magic Circle

www.themagiccircle.com
Tel. (011) 44-20-738-2222
12 Stephenson Way
London NW12HD
United Kingdom

The premier home of magic in the United Kingdom, this century-old club is open to members on Monday afternoon and evening. At certain times of the year shows are given for the public; otherwise, the club is closed to non-members. There are also an extensive museum and library. Members receive *The Magic Circular*, the oldest magazine in magic, and there are lectures and shows presented throughout the year.

The Magic Circle also has a "Young Magicians Club" with its own magazine.

GLOSSARY

Magician's Lingo

Magicians use lots of odd words as shortcuts when referring to things in their world. Here are some helpful examples.

Convincer: A physical or psychological bit of business that adds an extra layer of conviction to a spectator's belief.

Crimp: A corner of a card that has been bent slightly so it can be located in the deck with a cut.

Double-backed card: A playing card that has a back on both sides (and, therefore, no face).

Double lift: The secret lifting and holding of two cards as one.

Effect: A trick. This has two more complex meanings for magicians: (1) An effect is a trick with a single magical happening. (2) This is what the spectators see, as in, "The effect from the audience's point of view."

Equivoque: A technique of verbal control where the spectator believes he or she is making free choices when, in fact, you are controlling his or her choices (also known as "magician's choice").

Force: Making a spectator select an item that you want him or her to pick. The spectator believes that it's a free choice.

Glimpse: A method for secretly peeking at a card somewhere in the deck—it can be on the top, bottom, or in the middle.

Internet magic shop: An online website where you can purchase magic props by mail order. Many of these now incorporate video demonstrations of many of their products.

Key card: A card whose identity is known to the magician, either because it has been glimpsed or the corner has been bent (crimped) and that can be positioned next to a chosen card so that it can later be found.

Magic shop: A physical place where you can see magic tricks demonstrated and get advice from the salesperson before you buy.

Magician's choice: See Equivoque.

Mathematical card trick: A card trick based entirely on hidden mathematical principles rather than sleight of hand.

Misdirection: What a magician does to draw the audience's attention away from a secret maneuver. It can be either physical or psychological misdirection.

Patter: What magicians say during a trick, that is, a script.

Royal flush: The highest-value hand you can have in a game of five-card poker.

Set-up: Something you do in advance of performing a trick. The set-up is a secret from the audience.

Time misdirection: Using time to create misdirection. When you change the spectators' focus, they will not remember the exact way something was by the time you redirect their attention toward it.

Trick: The magical thing a magician does. There are two essential kinds of tricks: effects and routines. An effect has a single magical event, whereas a routine has several magical events. This is a different definition of routine than the verb used when magicians talk about "routining magic," which involves the careful creation of a show in which multiple tricks are performed in a thoughtful and dramatically interesting order.

INDEX

INDEX

INDEX

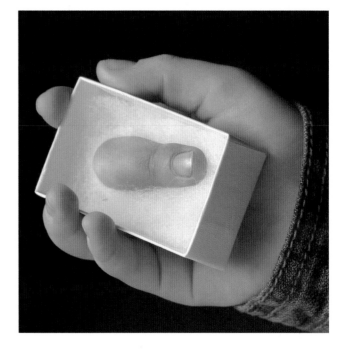
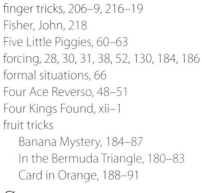

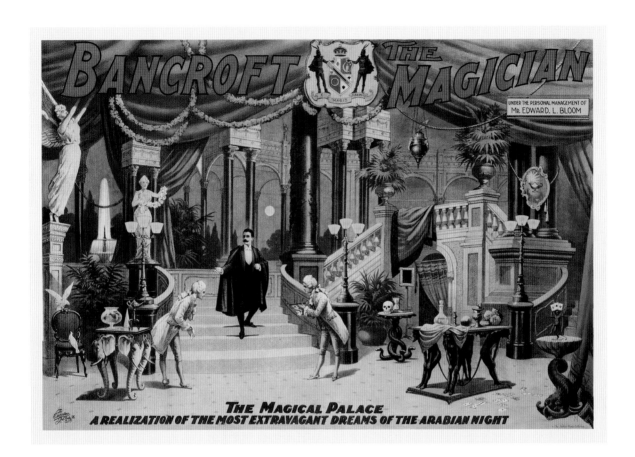